GO big

Matthew Burton

Illustrations by
Chris Madden

wren
&rook

First published in Great Britain in 2020 by Wren & Rook

ISBN: 978 1526362353
E-book ISBN: 978 1526362360

10 9 8 7 6 5 4

FSC

Wren & Rook
An imprint of
Hachette Children's Group
Part of Hodder & Stoughton
Carmelite House
50 Victoria Embankment
London EC4Y 0DZ

An Hachette UK Company
www.hachette.co.uk
www.hachettechildrens.co.uk

Publishing Director: Debbie Foy
Senior Editor: Laura Horsley
Art Director: Laura Hambleton
Designed by Claire Yeo

Printed in the United Kingdom

For my lovely Laura, Olivia and Theo. You make the good times even better, and the worst worth battling through. I could not love you more.

CONTENTS

Part 3: CONQUERING CHALLENGES

Part 4: LEAPING INTO THE FUTURE

Conclusion

INTROD

UCTION

School – the best days of your life. That's what everyone says, isn't it? If only it was as simple as that. You might love it (I hope you do). But as you make the next step to secondary school, or if you're already there and settling in, you *might* be feeling overwhelmed or any mixture of bonkers emotions.[1] Some people will love the idea of making new friends and moving round a brand new, shiny building[2] with a different teacher for every lesson. However, some people can't think of anything they would rather do less, and crave legging it over the fence (never EVER do this) and heading home to have a relaxing afternoon on their PlayStation.

Whatever ideas, fears, hopes and nightmares are bouncing around your mind right now, though, know this: it's going to be fine. You are going to be fine. Better than that: you are going to *excel*. Let's dismantle those worries, one by one, and start to look forward to what's to come … and that is a world of amazing experiences, brilliant people you haven't yet met, and lots of incredible opportunities for your future.

[1] Happy and sad and scared and amazed and a little bit fascinated, all at the same time, is completely okay.
[2] Not all schools are brand new, or shiny … Some even have holes in the roof and buckets in the corridors where water is dripping down from the roof. But some are just B-E-A-UTIFUL!

But I know what I'd be thinking if I were you right at this point. I'd be thinking:

Why on EARTH would I listen to YOU? You're old. Proper old.[3]

As old as a fossil? Maybe. But like most people, this old fossil went to school and though I enjoyed it, on the whole, it doesn't mean I didn't struggle with some parts of it. Then after progressing through the years, finishing my exams, leaving school and going to university, I decided to go back

[3] That would be unfair though. I arrived on this planet after the dinosaurs did but before mobile phones so I'm not that old. Older than you, but probably younger than your great-grandparents. I'd call it late twenties (but that would be a lie, seeing as I'm 36). Anyway ...

to secondary school to become an English teacher. Since then, I've taught thousands of brilliant young 'uns[4] – some for whom school was a walk in the park on a summer's day, and some for whom it was a hike through treacle in a blizzard. I've seen the highs, the lows, the tears, the smiles, and everything in between. I'm now a head teacher and absolutely **LOVE** the job. My hope is that you can benefit from my experiences and those of the people I know, so that you can absolutely smash your first few years at school.

I've written this book for you, so that whenever you feel worried or overwhelmed by school, you can dip in and find the answers you need. Think of it as your partner in crime[5] or a friend sitting on the shelf who you can shout at when you need something. Can I predict how it's going to go for you, _____[6]? No. There are a million things that could happen. But I hope these tips and hints nudge you on the right path and, if there's nothing else working for you, make you feel as if there's someone in your corner, with a bit of advice. My aim is to introduce you to (or help you along with)

[4] That's Yorkshire for 'children' and 'teenagers'.
[5] Though don't commit any crimes AT ALL.
[6] I've left a blank here for you to write your own name so you have a special personalised copy. You're welcome! Don't do that if you've just flicked to this page in a bookshop though. Or if you've borrowed it from someone. Or if it's a library copy …

something that is fantastic. Something magical. Something so staggeringly, awesomely incredible that soon your world will probably be transformed so that, even if you're still longing for primary school, it will feel like that terrifying yet brilliant moment you first went on a rollercoaster – a moment after realising you've just drunk an entire strawberry milkshake and your stomach was a little 'unstable'. You felt nervous, then very sick and slightly scared, but after a few minutes you were having the most incredible time and didn't want it to end.[7]

Don't get me wrong, secondary school takes some people longer to adapt to than others, and sometimes you will feel sad. That's normal. That's life. At primary school, you'd probably been at the same school for years, known your teachers' pets' cousins' middle names and been able to dodge all the holes and grates in the playground with your eyes closed. It might even have felt like your second home. But at secondary school, you're leaving that all behind for a completely new place, with a new massive playground, and suddenly your assemblies have trebled in size. Corridors can seem wide, the other children (including those huge 'children' in sixth form who drive a car to school) can be a bit intimidating to start with, and friendships you used to have won't always be the same. But just because the kids are older it doesn't mean they won't look out for you. Friendships might change but you'll make lots of new ones too. You might even fall in love, you might fall out of love; you might realise

[7] This time, though, hopefully the person in front of you won't be covered with the second appearance of a pink milkshake.

that you're not who you thought you were. But whatever your own personal journey – I'm here to help you get there, make it happen and be the best you can be. Activist and Nobel Peace Prize laureate, Malala Yousafzai once said,

'ONE CHILD, ONE TEACHER, ONE BOOK, ONE PEN CAN CHANGE THE WORLD.'

Malala Yousafzai –
Pakistani activist for female education and the youngest
Nobel Peace Prize laureate

When Malala says something, we listen. I listen, you listen, and, quite frankly, the world should listen. She's someone who battled oppression, terror and evil to stand up for her right to get an education, and we certainly need to understand why she fought so strongly. She believes that anyone – you, me, that person on the bus who goes to the secondary down the road – can change the world. The power of education to help you do that is massive. It opens doors that we thought were locked; it gives us the bricks to build the highest tower from which we can see the beauty of the world. Or, to put it without using metaphors, a good education can help you to get the life you want for yourself. I think it's one of our responsibilities to leave the world in a slightly better place than we found it, and you getting the education you are entitled to is a massive part of that.

Let's fast-forward a few years. It's a Thursday morning in late August and you're about to collect your final exam results. You're now the oldest student in the school. Your stomach's rumbling. Your hands are a bit sweaty and you feel pretty sick (we'll go into this again later, too). Whenever anyone gets to this moment in their lives, it's easy to forget what's important. In this moment (and every other tense and nervy moment throughout school), you need to do the following very simple thing. Ask yourself: have I done my best, and did I give it everything?

If the answer to both questions is yes, then nobody will ever, ever complain. Everything is going to be fine and you will have a great future ahead of you. Have a read of this book and let's have a chat about a few truths/lies/worries/hopes/fears that everyone has when landing at secondary school – when your wheels have hit the runway but you can't touch down smoothly just yet. Within a few pages, we'll have you showing your passport, collecting your bags and emerging out into arrivals with a huge grin on your face.

On th
Way

e

Up

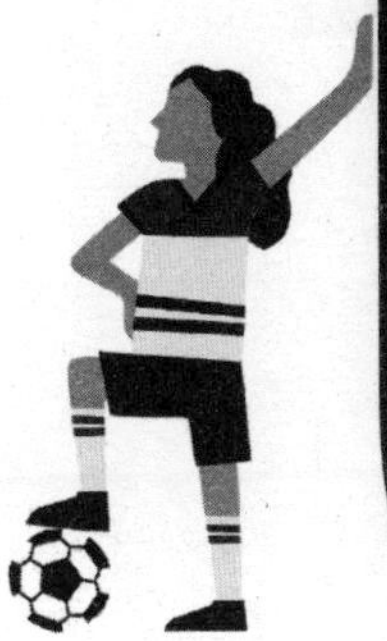

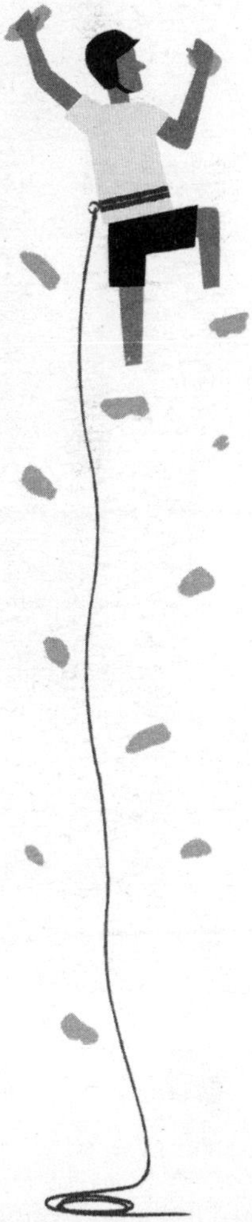

THE
BIG
STEP

Throughout our lives we go through all sorts of changes, or what we call 'transitions'. We might move house or decide not to eat meat any more and become vegetarian.[1] One of the biggest transitions any of us will go through, though, is the leap from primary to secondary school. If you're already at secondary school then you can jump right past this part of the book and land on the next section because you've made it – HURRAH! But if you're in your last few years of primary school, this is for you.

The first you heard about the next step in your education journey would probably have been a few years ago, when the older kids in school – so sophisticated, grown up and mature – left the primary for a day and went to the secondary school up the road. Your school fell eerily quiet. Tumbleweed blew through the corridors. Break time was strangely empty. It was a bit, well, odd. When the older kids came back the next day (for a couple of weeks afterwards until the summer holidays, anyway), it felt like order was restored.

But your transition from primary to secondary school will actually begin much earlier than you might think, and your

[1] Or switch from an Android to an iPhone. A big life decision I'm sure you'll agree ...

schools and teachers will be working together to ensure you are completely prepared. You need to know that you're going to the right place, your parents or guardians are happy with it and you have someone you can speak to if you are at all worried. The last thing anyone wants is for your first half term to be full of

 'Oh nooo, what have I DONE?'

moments. Schools want you to go there, but you need to know that it's the right place for you first, as do your folks.

That's why what's called 'transition' starts really early. I'm not talking about newborns doing algebra or scholarships being given out to kids on the back of a good finger painting in nursery. But early enough so that you're ready and can get it right from the start.

TASTER SESSIONS

Sometimes schools will run 'taster' sessions, even when you're only seven or eight, but the main stuff will usually start in the year before you leave school. You might get invites to a load of open evenings and a taster day up at the local secondary. Teachers and kids might also pop down to your place to speak to you about what goes on there, what they think of it and the opportunities you'll get. Sometimes children will come and deliver some sessions in music, sports, drama or dance (or anything else, actually), so you can get a feeling for the ethos of the school.

When you're invited to stuff, my advice is this:

Go.
And.
Do it.

Even if your family has been going to the same school for the last 15 generations and your great, great, great (you get the picture) great-grandad who was a caveman and founder of the place and won 'Best Cave Painting' in 1278 BCE, it's still really important that the school you pick is right for **YOU**.

Open evenings are fun, too. You're not daft, I know, so I probably don't need to tell you this, but I will anyway. If the school puts pâté on toast on in the French department, is re-enacting the Big Bang in science and has a range of children who appear to be professional musicians rehearsing a full opera in the music department, I think you know that isn't exactly how *every* day is going to be. There are a great number of days at school when it won't be anything like that. In fact, it might be quite – dare I say it – *boring*. Not as in falling-asleep-in-lessons boring, but in the sense that you'll go to school, have some lessons, learn some stuff, see your friends and go home. That's why you need to go through a load of open evenings and get to the root of the issue: in which one of the schools you visit can you see yourself being most happily bored on *those* days?[2] Who are the people to help you cut through it? Which corridors feel comfortable? Can you imagine yourself there? Can you look into the future and see yourself happy in those buildings, with those people, for **FIVE** long **YEARS**?

[2] You know the ones I mean. You wake up – the sky's grey. You go to pour your cereal and the box is empty. You stub your toe leaving the house. You have PE (outside) and it's cold (and raining), and you've got a headache. Your bus is also late and you have a load of homework due, which you haven't done. And you just don't want to get started on Eeeeenglish – EUGH.

You could even (if you're super-organised) set up a spreadsheet where you mark loads of schools against things that are important to you out of ten. For example:

- *Warmth of the welcome – were people 'nice'?* 7/10
- *What were the students like? Did you meet any? Did they help you out?* 6/10
- *What was the building like? Can you see yourself 'fitting in'?* 8/10
- *What's the journey there and back like from home? Did it take you 17 hours and mean you needed to swim across a river to get there?* 7/10

Count up your scores and have a look at what comes first. Even once you've had a look around, don't decide then. It might be like a bolt of lightning[3] and you might just know, but it's more likely that you'll have a couple of schools in contention. That's why it's important that you have a look early. But whatever you do, choose a school because it's right for you, not because your best friends are going there. There could be a particular school for performing arts, for example, and you may **REALLY** fancy going but none of your friends are. Would you be happy knowing that you didn't give it a go

[3] Though I hope not, as that could hurt.

just because your mates weren't? For these sorts of decisions, a big cup of tea, the biscuit tin and a chat with your family around the kitchen table might be needed.

All these options and decisions might sound great, but if you live somewhere with only one secondary school nearby and there aren't lots to choose from, then don't worry. Find things out about that school early and talk to those lovely people inside it – whether it's a friend's older siblings, students or teachers at the open day. They'll want to help you and make sure you're feeling good about the time you're going to spend inside those walls learning loads of fantastic things. Any questions you have, just ask them.

DECISION TIME

Your last year at primary school will soon come around, and then it truly will be decision time. Some schools need you to do an exam before you go in (an 'entry exam'), but a lot will just need your mum and/or dad or lovely person you live with to send a form off (or do it online), and then you wait. And wait ... and wait ... and wonder whether you've got the school you want.[4] And then you'll find out! Hopefully (and for most people), it will be good news, and the secondary school you chose will come through,[5] but there is the odd occasion when it doesn't.

If it does, brilliant. If it doesn't, don't worry. Have a look back at that spreadsheet and have a think about the good bits of the one you've been given. All schools have their strengths and their bits that people would like to be better, and it might end up suiting you more. The world has a funny way of sorting things out for people and you might find the school you really didn't want is actually the perfect place for you after all.

---

[4] But don't worry about it – once it's sent, there's nothing more you can do!
[5] BUT WOULDN'T IT BE SO MUCH MORE INTERESTING IF THE HOGWARTS SORTING HAT GOT INVOLVED? That would be just magical.

TRANSITION

From the day your letter comes through,[6] your transition begins. Slowly, though. It's not like you're trying to set a new land speed record and be there in full uniform every single day before you start. This is the point at which, if you're worried about something, you should ask. Get your folks to drop the school an email and put your mind at rest. Check out the school website and social media feeds: really get a taste of what's to come for you in the next few years.

Exciting, Isn't it?

At some point you and everyone in your class (and year) will go off (usually for a day) to try out their new schools – you included. This is a transition day – it could be called other things, but it's basically the day that most people at the end of primary school will spend in their new secondary school

---

[6] And again, sadly not like Harry Potter. There will be no large man on a flying motorcycle delivering an enchanted letter to you. Unless the postal service in certain parts of the world is different to what it is in the UK.

– and it will be a nervy one. It's natural! You're meeting the people you'll spend a **LOT** of time with over the next few years – some of whom you will meet for the first time on that day! You'll spend time with your new teachers and meet the important people who'll be there to help you out during that first week as you get lost after PE and think you've been abandoned by all of mankind when actually your classroom is just next door.[7] You'll probably spend time in an assembly, do some work with your new form (yes, there will be people from other schools you will need to talk to at some point), and you might get into a few lessons to see the sorts of things you'll be doing. You'll also find out the **MOST** important thing: where the canteen is and how you get your food. You can't do the business in your lessons if there's no fuel in the engine!

After that you'll fly through the last few weeks at primary school – graduations, parties, proms, barbecues, sunshine, tears, leaving day, hugs – and then it's summer. Saying goodbye will be emotional – and those tears might be happy or sad or a mixture of both – but this isn't the end destination; it's just the next stop on the journey. As you leave the primary school gates for the last time, your teachers will be so proud of who you've become and they'll be excited to hear about how things are going in your next stage. It might feel sad to say farewell to those friends who aren't going 'up' with you too, but stay in contact so you can share stories in the future.

[7] You might arrive all hot and sweaty and worried but it's FINE!

PREPARING FOR THE MOVE

Teachers know it's summer because the shops start with those enormous **'BACK TO SCHOOL!'** signs[8] with backwards chalk-style letters on a blackboard,[9] which is your chance to start shopping and preparing. Now, your parents aren't daft. They'll try to get away with buying one blazer that will see you all the way through secondary school. It'll be like a tent your entire family (and a passing travelling circus) could sleep in to start with, and they'll have the idea that 'you'll grow into it'. Every parent does it, so you're not alone. But before you go shopping –

find out what the uniform rules are!

[8] Which is the worst. Students and teachers work really hard through the year. Then we reach that lovely day at the end of term when the sky is blue, the holidays are here, the ice creams are flowing, and teachers (sometimes) end up dancing on tables with the caretaker they've never actually spoken to but once stole milk from in the staffroom fridge. And then they wake up the morning after and the local clothes shop is doing '3 for 2' on white shirts with a picture of a really happy looking child. All of this before they've had the chance to even think about their summer holiday ... Completely THE WORST.

[9] Do you even know what a blackboard *is*? I'm not even sure I remember them. I think they went out around the time of the Victorians. But some shops *still* think they're in schools!

If you need black shoes, buy a pair of *black shoes*. Trainers aren't shoes. Just like golf clubs aren't shoes and smelly, French mouldy cheese isn't shoes (though it smells like shoes when people don't wear socks). So buy black shoes. If it says black trousers, then black skinny jeans aren't allowed. And if it says that you're not allowed nose piercings, don't go and get a nose piercing a week before you go back. It won't be the best start. Think about things like your hair, too – if you make the creative decision to go for a cherry-red mohawk with your favourite singer's lyrics shaved into the sides the weekend before you start back, then check that you're allowed such a 'do'. Obviously, I don't want to be a total buzzkill. You should express yourself, and you'll find more on this and how you should embrace and love every part of yourself, even the bits that other people might think are 'weird', in chapter five (turn to page 67). But you do have to stick to the rules. All schools will be different but if you make a good start of it, then you'll absolutely fly.

MR BURTON'S FIRST DAY PREPARATION CHECKLIST

Uniform: shirt, trousers/skirt, blazer and shoes all checked against the school's rules	
PE kit	
Equipment basics – pen, pencil, ruler, rubber	
School bag	
Lunch (have you packed your sandwiches or are you having school dinner?)	
A plan for how you're going to get to school	
A big breakfast on your first morning (but try to have breakfast every morning – it will kick-start your day!)	

YOUR FIRST DAY

It's time to start! All that preparation is finally going to pay off as you walk into your new school. Now, your first day's going to be a mixture of things:

Excitement.
Worry.
Fear.
Anticipation.
Hunger ...

It won't necessarily be what will soon become a 'normal' day – there'll be tours, new books, new teachers, new people, lost bags, **MASSIVE** playgrounds, **ENORMOUS** older kids, and there might not actually be any lessons – but you've done it. You've started. You're off and running!

Of course, everyone's first day is going to be different. You might be going to the school where all of your friends and your siblings are, and where your mum is the head teacher. So it's literally the least scary day you've ever known. If that's you, brilliant, enjoy it. But remember that if you *do* know nearly everyone, it might be comfortable and feel great, but there will be someone who doesn't know anyone. The world needs more kindness in it, so make sure you ask people's names, push yourself to say hello (even though it's an **'OHMYGODICAN'TBELIEVEYOUTALKEDTOHIMYOUDON'T EVENKNOWHIMOHMYGODYOUARESOBRAVE'** situation) and try to be the best version of you.

On the other hand, you might be the person who has to travel miles and miles to get to school. You might need to get a lift, then a train, then a bus and then walk – and once you arrive, you don't know anyone. If that's you, don't fear. While there will be a lot of stuff you're worrying about, this is a **BRILLIANT** chance to really stamp your mark on your own life and say: **'THIS IS THE PERSON I WANT TO BE!'** Be brave and talk to people. Making new friends is amazing, and schools are all set up to help you move around in the circles where you'll find people of your age, with your ambitions, and who are your type of people. Meeting new people is fantastic and there aren't many times in life that you get the chance to start again completely, while still being allowed to keep hold of everything you like about the 'old' you. So you can still be friends with those people you used to play footy with (and you can still play footy with them too), it's just that you can get another group of mates who play a different sport, too. Who knows – those new friends could help you unearth a skill you never knew you had!

Whoever you are, and however many people you know or don't know, just remember: be nice, be positive and remember that every single person – even your teacher – is nervous and wants this to go well. They have to work with you for five years, too, and nobody wants five years of weirdness, awkwardness or difficulty. Ask teachers things, and throw yourself into your new school. You won't regret it. There's a saying that goes 'you only get one chance to make a first impression' and I can guarantee you that every single person at school – teachers, cleaners, caretakers, lunchtime staff, teaching assistants and everyone else – love to see kindness and a sense that you are interested in what they have to say. Even if it isn't the school you chose, give them a chance – they are very likely to prove themselves to you. They want to make it work for you.

MR BURTON'S FIRST DAY AT SCHOOL ...

My first day at secondary school was *terrifying*. I remember walking up in the rain, my skin uncomfortable and my pulse throbbing in my head. I also remember, really clearly, walking into the school and wondering where all these people had come from. I felt scared, nervous and alone to begin with ... and then things started. My teachers made it easy to meet people from other schools, and I quickly became more comfortable. The uniform, though: that was strange. It was thick and uncomfortable, and I felt it looked daft (even though there were thousands of others in it!).[10] After worrying that every teacher was suspiciously human-like, and wondering when they would start to SHOUT AT THE TOP OF THEIR VOICES AND MAKE MY LIFE A MISERY, I started to realise that maybe, just maybe, this

[10] I couldn't deal with the tie AT ALL. Although I did feel like I ran a huge multinational business because I was wearing one.

might be okay. As it turns out, it was – and I went back to work in a school, too!

The next 'first day at school' I had was as a teacher, and let me tell you: THAT WAS A HUNDRED TIMES MORE SCARY! Meeting my new form was just so terrifying and amazing that I struggled to even string a sentence together. They fired questions at me, parents called me to ask me stuff (and my voice did that thing where it went high for a second because I was nervous), and I didn't really know the answers. I was new, just like my students were. But I soon got into the swing of things, and it must have gone okay – I ended up keeping the form for five years!

So never, ever think that you're on your own at the start of a new term. Loads and loads of schools have got brand new teachers starting their first ever teaching jobs on the day you're starting at that school (they're called NQTs or Newly Qualified Teachers), and they'll *definitely* be feeling just like you are. Every other person in your form is feeling the same, too. Some people are just much better at hiding it!

GET
LOST

There are small secondary schools and there are big secondary schools but, more often than not, the building you'll be spending the next few years of your life in will be a whole lot bigger than your primary school. It can feel like a bit of a maze in more ways than one, and when I talk to people who are a few weeks into school and are now confidently sashaying from lesson to lesson like they're on *Strictly Come Dancing*, one of the biggest fears they can remember is that of being lost.

Now, 'lost' doesn't just mean not being able to find your way around. That's easily solvable. Plenty of people are there to help with that – you'll have tours and there will be helpers, teachers and older students to aid you in getting from A to B. Don't worry about asking. Generally, human beings are lovely and want to help you get around. People get it: you're new and you're still figuring it all out.

But there might also come a time in that first week – which will feel about a month long and ten seconds long at the very same time – when you might have a little bit of a reminisce[1]

[1] I'm sure you do know what that means, but in case you don't, it means looking back with fondness. Like when you look at those brown and wrinkled old pictures of smartly dressed people from generations ago in your family. Or looking back at that time on the rollercoaster with the strawberry milkshake and smiling (before you remember the bit where you ... oh no, not that bit ...).

about 'the good old days' at primary school, and how you wish it was this time last year when you only had one classroom to remember and you were the oldest at break time.[2] It's understandable and completely expected – you're at a new school and it can all feel quite alien. But never, ever feel like you're alone. Even if you are the only person starting that day in the second year because one of your parents got a new job at the other end of the country, people have the exact same fears that you do. Here are my top tips to navigate that feeling of being in a maze (in many ways) in those first few days of secondary school:

✫ 1) Ask your way around

Pretty simple, isn't it? If you're stuck, ask people. Ninety-nine times out of a hundred, they'll be lovely, kind and helpful – and if you're unlucky enough to pick that one person who's not very nice, then ask someone else. Most people will point you in the right direction and might even give you a personal escort to your next lesson, and then, as an added bonus, you can count on them for a kind word when you next see them in the corridor.

✫ 2) Accept help and find your 'go-to'

Things won't get better – neither your worries nor being

---

[2] It might even have been called 'play time'. I remember talking about 'play time' when I was 15 and my friends never let me get away with it. They still mention it now ...

'geographically challenged' – if you don't firstly admit that you need a helping hand, and then accept one when it's offered. Your teachers will ask you a million times if you're all right and whether you need a hand – and **THEY MEAN IT!** Take the help. These are people who have been to school themselves. They've done all the falling out with friends and the failed young romances. They've experienced the heartache of not getting the grades they wanted, and the weird feeling of turning into an adult with the anger and sadness and happiness all at the same time, and just wanting to shout,

'Aaargh! Everyone is an idiot and nobody understands me!'

at the wall. They've already navigated the waves of results day and sailed on to the (slightly) calmer seas of being a young adult. They really know their stuff and can help you.

Yes, some teachers might come across as 'scary' when you first meet them. Some might come across as 'funny' or even 'sooo embarrassing'. But that's okay because they're not going to become your best pal. In fact, they're looking after you even when you don't realise it – and teachers are trained to keep you safe *all the time*. They'll be there through the best and worst, the highs and lows, and the (happy and sad) tears of the next few years. We've got you!

There may be some teachers you just don't get on with and those you think are completely brilliant. And there'll likely be one who becomes your 'go-to' for when you need help. Everyone has 'go-to' people in their life. So if you fall out with someone, who do you tell to make you feel better again? Or if something happens that makes you feel bad, who do you ask for support from? You'll have your people at home. You'll have your mates from primary school. In fact, if I asked you to tell me right now who your 'go-to' person is in school, I bet you could. (Don't, because I can't hear you and you're reading a book. Especially if you're reading this in the dead of night and you share a room with your sister or something ...) Anyway, the point is

➡ **Find that person**

at your new school. There are times when you'll need an adult, for advice or help, so take some time to think about who that is. Don't force it; you'll realise who that person is (or people, as there are very likely to be **LOADS** of them) really quickly, and the first few days you spend meeting your form tutor, teachers, head of year, head teacher and everyone else in school will give you a good idea of who you think it might be.

Then ask them things, tell them what's up and understand that they won't judge you if you're a crying mess. They just want you to be okay, and (pssst ... secret), they're not going to be annoyed with you if they're not your 'go-to' for the whole time in school. You'll change and adapt, become more confident and have setbacks along the way. All the while, though, those humans at school are there for you: use them wisely!

⭐ 3) Be honest

Some people will start secondary school and use every opportunity on social media and in real life to talk about how much 'I **LOVE** it' and 'I'm so good at geography and I'm in the top set and I've got loads of friends and I can't even believe I even hung around with those BABIES in primary because, oh, I'm *so* sophisticated now'. The reality is that, while some of what people say may be true, it's best to understand 'Mr Burton's Very Scientific Rule of Reality about What People Say When They're Trying to Look Good and You're Not Feeling Very Confident Yourself'.[3]

[3] It's very scientific. I can't believe I'm even talking about it in a book for young people. The level of science involved is frankly staggering.

Here goes:

1) Listen to what they say, for example:

'I LOVE secondary school, I have so many friends and am never ever worried about my exams.'

2) Understand what they say
3) Accept that they might feel like that but that you don't and that's okay
4) Go about your own day and don't let it affect you

Remember, we're all going to face tough times. They come at different stages, and those who are chiming on about how easy secondary school is might not actually be finding it quite as easy as they say they are.

Be open – tell people what you're thinking right now and be honest!

✯ 4) Do your research!

If you're someone who really struggles with directions, with forgetting stuff and being unable to remember where to go, then how do you get better at it? Training! If you *know* that the walk from science to technology is going to be a *nightmare* next week, then train yourself and do the route a few times during lunchtime. One of your mates might be in that class – tag along with them when they're doing the route for the first time and, slowly but surely, you'll get it!

⭐ 5) Make sure you have your Triangle of Trust

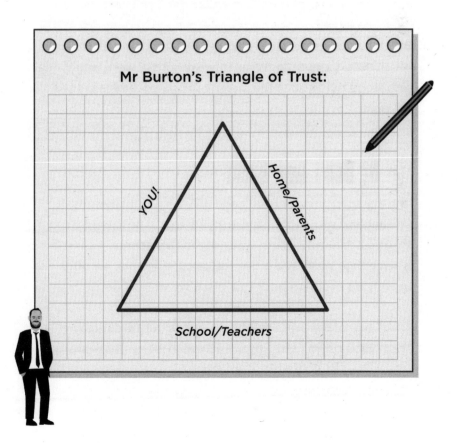

Mr Burton's Triangle of Trust:

YOU!

Home/parents

School/Teachers

The Triangle of Trust is really important – and if home, school and you are working together, you'll be strong. Sometimes we all need a bit of extra help, and that's fine; it doesn't make you any less likely to be an amazing success in this school or in the future. But you do need to talk about it to make things get better. Just open your cake hole[4] and **LET US KNOW WHAT'S UP.**

You are a huge part of it. One whole third of it! Without you, it falls down. It's just two sticks dangling in mid-air. **DO YOUR BIT!** It's proper science (it's actually not), but it makes sense – we all need to work together to make school work, and if one side stops trying, then that means things become a bit of a struggle.

✵ 6) Don't look back!

Primary school might have been great, your final exams brilliant and you might have enjoyed your time there *far more* than you think you'll ever enjoy secondary school. As humans, when things go wrong or we feel uncomfortable, we often like to wish we could go back to a place we've felt happy.

That's one of the reasons why we watch our favourite film 12-squillion times (and why we all watch *Harry Potter* every

---

[4] My mum used to say that to me (referring to what is more commonly known as my mouth). Usually when she was politely requesting me to close it ...

Sunday afternoon back to back throughout November and December because it's **NEARLY CHRISTMAAAS – HURRAH!**). It's why we like a particular flavour of ice cream or why your folks might choose the same holiday destination every year. It's because it's comfortable and, because our first memories of it are good, then part of going back to it is about remembering those times and trying to create more of those memories. If your only taste of ice cream had been petrol flavour,[5] do you think you'd want to go back and have some more? NO!

In this case, going back to primary school isn't an option. And that's a good thing. You're at a new, exciting stage of your life. So we need to look at what we've got and make sure it works for us. Looking back might make us feel better in the short-term, but it doesn't help us find our new path in the long-term.

Whatever your experience, there are plenty of teachers, parents, resources and friends around you to help. Be brave, be bold, be the 'secondary school' you, and you will be

---

[5] I actually saw some advertised once in an ice cream shop. I am pretty sure it was either just a controversial name (so people go, 'OOOH, *THAT* sounds different! Shall we get some, Neil?') and it's actually just liquorice or something, or it was lost in translation. Either way, I didn't buy it.

MYTHS, RUMOURS AND SECRETS: WHAT REALLY HAPPENS AT SECONDARY SCHOOL

3

Parents and students often ask me[1] whether the 'rumours' about secondary school are true. When I ask them what those 'rumours' are, they're very often the same ones that I spent time worrying about when I was a young chap, just about to make the jump up to secondary.

While I can't promise you that these things won't happen – and I'm sure somewhere in the world, on one day, maybe even a hundred years ago, some of them did – what I can say with a reasonable amount of confidence is that

these things will not happen to you.

Let's dispose of them one by one:

[1] I don't know why they ask me – do they think I'm some kind of teacher or something?!

MR BURTON'S MYTHS AND LEGENDS

✮ 1) I'll have my head flushed down the toilet every day

First things first – think of a toilet. No toilet I have ever seen in my life has the capacity for the average 11-year-old's head to fit in it.[2] On top of this, never in my whole life have I heard of this actually happening to anyone in a school I've gone to as a student, a school I've worked in, a school I've visited, or any other place where young people come together.

✮ 2) I'll be bullied every minute of every day

I can safely say you won't get bullied every minute of every day. But I can't say bullying will never happen, so if you do experience it, tell someone you trust who can help you (find out more in chapter eight on page 101). It's fixable. And it's absolutely not embarrassing. Every single person at some point in their life at secondary school will feel like they're being picked on for *something*. I certainly did. The myth,

---

[2] Unless it's one of those Italian toilets with a very large hole in the ground, but still … how many schools have those?

though, that you'll be relentlessly bullied from minute one to minute 351,000[3] is not true.

✬ 3) The teachers are horrible and just out to 'get' children

Not true. Not one little bit. Teachers spend years and years working hard, dedicating their entire working lives to being in schools to help children. Teachers are teachers – primary or secondary – and they are full of helpfulness, inspiration and love for their subject. Do you reckon anyone would go to school, then to sixth form, then to university and then *choose* to go back to school for their *entire career* if they just wanted to pick on people for a job? Naaah, mate. They want you to love their subject like they do, and they want to pass on what they know and bring nuclear physics, netball, Kandinsky, Brecht or Pythagoras to life for you in the way that someone did for them.

✬ 4) I'll be able to go home if the weather gets too hot

Every year, as soon as the sun shines, this comes out. No.

---

[3] Calculated on a five-year secondary school career, with 195 days per year and six hours per day (9 a.m. till 3 p.m.), and every hour having 60 minutes.

⭐ 5) I'll be able to go home if the weather gets too cold

Every year, as soon as a single flake of snow falls, this comes out. No.[4]

⭐ 6) I'll be doing exams every single day

You won't – exams and tests are part of school, but the *most* important thing is learning what you are taught (let's call it the 'stuff').

Exams are just a part of checking how much you know about that stuff.

An exam that doesn't go all that well is *not* the end of the world; it's just showing that you've still got some stuff to learn!

[4] There might be the *occasional* day when this happens, but it is *very, very* unlikely.

✯ 7) I'll get 35,643,654 hours of homework every single night

Not true. Homework is important, but you will get an amount that is right for you at that time in your school life. It's supposed to sit along with what you're doing in your lessons to help it move into your long-term memory,[5] and teachers will plan it so that it helps to nail down what you've learnt that day or that week. It also might be used to test you on something you did a while ago – a massive part of remembering the stuff you need to know is actually forgetting it and then forcing yourself to recall it. Homework might be linked to that in various subjects. You'll get an amount you can manage, and it's best to do it when you get it, so you can keep on top of it.

✯ 8) Nobody will understand me or 'get' me

A big concern people have is that nobody will be on their team or squad – or nobody will be their type of person. But even if you're the only one going to the secondary school from your class, you *will* build up those friendships (more of this in chapter seven on page 85). School will support you with that, and don't forget, you're all in a very similar situation.

---

[5] The part of the brain that is like that wardrobe in your house where you keep all your dressing-up outfits from when you were little, your old toys and reports from when you were in Reception saying things like, 'He can now pick up a spoon with his hand!' Things that are supposed to be remembered for a long time are kept there, and they need to be returned to quite often so that those memories are still sparked when you pull out your old Buzz Lightyear mask or that photo of you that is OH MY GOODNESS, SO EMBARRASSING dressed like a carrot in a nativity play when you were five.

✦ 9) I won't get the special help I was getting at primary school because the teachers there were nice and you're all AWFUL!

If you get some extra help – one-to-one support with someone, help with reading or writing – your secondary school will know about it. Every school will have someone who makes sure people with extra needs are looked after properly, and your primary school support person will (very likely) already have spoken to your support person at secondary school, so they'll know what you get at the moment, how it works for you and what needs to happen in the future. If you need that help, you'll get that help!

WHAT WILL BE DIFFERENT

So, we've looked at some of the things people are scared of every year in every school, but what things will actually be different? Well ...

⭐ 1) Your year will grow

No, time won't expand. Don't worry about that. It's very, very likely, though, that your primary class will be tiny compared to your secondary one. It can be a bit scary, but it's also amazing to be a small fish in a bigger pond than before –

more room to swim and more fish to jump around with!

⚝ 2) Subjects are in different places

This is probably new. Every lesson will be in a different place. Different classes in different areas with different people, and they're all led by ...

⚝ 3) Different teachers

You will be surrounded by lots more teachers than before. These are people who chose to teach one particular subject, like history or maths.

They love it, they study it, they spend their weekends thinking about it and planning it.

They are the ultimate experts – so challenge them on what their favourite bit of knowledge is about their subject! They can and will fascinate you (or possibly bore you to sleep, depending on how fascinating the fact actually is – some facts are more interesting to different people than others, of course!).

✦ 4) Bigger (or smaller) classes

This one depends on where and when. You might have a small group for some subjects – maybe some catch-up reading or in practical classes where you're using tools – and bigger classes in other areas, but you'll certainly be in different lessons, with different people. It's a brilliant way to meet new people, really get to grips with some stuff that might be what you end up doing for a job in the future ... and it gives you some interesting tales to tell at break time when you meet up with your crew again!

MR BURTON'S
TOOLS
FOR SCHOOL

Now, as I've said before, secondary school is absolutely nothing to worry about, but there are things that can help you be a **HUGE** success. I don't mean a pen, pencil, rubber and all that jazz (although don't forget them), but I mean the 'personal' things you need to make your big leap into the unknown a great triumph.

✦ 1) Bouncebackability

We could go on for years and years about this, but if we're going to boil it down to one thing I think you *have* to work on, develop, practise, exercise and sharpen, it's this: bounce-backability. People call it various things – it can be known as 'resilience' or 'grit' or simply 'thatwasn'tveryniceorverygood butI'mnotgoingtogiveupI'mgoingtotryagain'.[1] If you work on this, everything else falls into place. Hard work, tolerance, openness and being a generally good egg[2] are all part of this. It's like the boss at the end of a level on your favourite game: if you can smash this one, then you can do the rest easily!

That said, bouncebackability isn't a particularly pleasant thing

---

[1] Yeah, simple, that one.
[2] Not literally an egg. Just a good person. A nice person. A quality human.

to have to practise, because it usually means that something has to have gone pretty wrong to be able to give it a go. Simply put, bouncebackability or 'resilience' is the ability of a person not to give up when something

goes
wrong.

Missed an open goal in PE and fallen over, ending up in a puddle of thick mud? Ignore the titters from that group of boys over there and have a go again.

Completely botched up a piece of French homework because you and verbs just don't seem to get on, so it's ended up making less than no sense whatsoever? Sit down, learn those verb forms and do it again.

Made a complete mess of what was, until now, a quite handsome-looking bookcase in technology, and now it resembles a broken piece of wood that looks like it's washed up on the side of a lake somewhere? Save what you can, don't give up, and make the thing again.

You see, bouncebackability is usually needed when you've put a load of time into something and the end result hasn't matched what you thought it would be. You thought you'd score that goal and knee slide through the mud like a footballing hero; you thought a French travel company would snap up your homework considering how good you *thought* it was; and you thought you might book a meeting with the chief executive of IKEA during the next school holiday about that quite *exceptional* bookcase so they could market it to the public worldwide. Instead, you were left a bit ... deflated.

The easy thing to do would be to say everyone else is wrong, insist you're right, refuse to take any feedback from anyone and keep doing what you're doing. The tough thing to do – and the whole point of bouncebackability – is to accept 'I wasn't very good' or 'that wasn't good enough' and that your efforts didn't match what came out in the end.

So if you fall off the horse, although it hurts, get back on.[3] Grit your teeth, wipe away the dust or dirt or tears, and think, *How can I make sure that doesn't happen next time?* Also consider what you've just learnt. Sometimes it might be a skill in a particular subject, and sometimes it might be something about you as a person. You're still learning, and you *will very probably* say a few things you shouldn't or do some daft things. We all make mistakes every day. So what? Learn from it, and let's make sure that the next time that open goal comes up, we absolutely smash the ball into the back of the net. And when we're next riding a horse, we don't fall off.[4]

[3] After being checked out by a trained medical practitioner first. If it's a real horse, and you've really fallen. It's a metaph— ... oh, don't worry. To be clear: IF YOU FALL OFF AN ACTUAL HORSE, SEE A DOCTOR BEFORE YOU GET BACK ON IT.
[4] Just remember to make sure you're fine to be on that horse after your previous fall. They are tall. Even ponies. Even unicorns.

✦ 2) Kindness

The other thing I think you probably already know – but is worth making really clear that *anyone*, in any part of the world, going into any job needs – is the following: just be nice. Everyone you know is going to get upset at some point; your body is going to do things over the next few years that you might have heard about but won't fully grasp until you experience it, and you probably won't enjoy school 100 per cent of the time. You will have days when you feel fed up, that your work's on top of you, and you panic about the future so much that you feel your breath almost being taken from your lungs.

Every single human being – you, me, that lady crossing the road with the sausage dog over there,[5] the Queen, your favourite vlogger, the boy in your class who's really good looking and has 32,856,238,958,673,295,723 Instagram followers and boasts of so many Snapchat streaks that it makes you green with jealousy, your teacher who appears happy every moment of every day – **EVERYONE** has worries of their own. People often don't want to talk about them, but they're there, and the *tiniest thing* we can do to make life a little bit easier for every single human being is give what costs nowt:[6] basic kindness. Unfortunately, we can't fix everything for everyone, but what we can do, and what we *should* do every day, hour, minute and second, is be kind.

[5] Awww! So cute, isn't it?
[6] Nothing. Nada. Nienté. Nul. Zero.

✧ 3) Effort and enthusiasm

Work hard. This sounds simple, and it sort of is. You won't do well without really rolling your sleeves up and grafting. There'll be homework you don't 'get' and there'll be teachers who give you a grade you don't think you deserve, with advice you don't agree with.

But don't give up.

Try talking in class as much as possible. Your teachers want you to talk, open up, show what you know, have a view on things and care about what's going on. Open your mouth and talk ... and if it's something you're not confident of saying in front of everyone else, don't worry: stick around at the end or go to see them at break time.

If you don't understand something at all, the chances are

that plenty of other people in your class don't either, and so it's probably your misconception[7] that everyone has understood it. Don't worry, a teacher isn't going to bite your head off[8] if you don't get it. What part of volcanoes don't you understand? What bit of simultaneous equations makes you feel like your brain is going to explode? You won't get told off for not 'getting it' – plenty of others don't, either, and your teacher will honestly be really pleased you've told them.

Football manager and former player Pep Guardiola once said,

'I WILL FORGIVE IF THE PLAYERS CANNOT GET IT RIGHT, BUT NOT IF THEY DO NOT TRY HARD.'

Josep "Pep" Guardiola – *Spanish Manager of Manchester City Football Club and former player*

[7] Something that you just don't understand or think the wrong thing about.
[8] Neither literally nor metaphorically, thank goodness.

Nothing comes easy, and your exams won't be completed by a magical flying pen that scores you full marks in a few years' time. Mistakes will be made on the way too. But you're going to have to breathe deeply, put the effort in, be enthusiastic when you can and get it done. Once you're there, you'll be glad you did. You're going to have a brilliant few years.

Be nice, work hard, bounce back, and all will be fine. Go get 'em!

Gett

Comfo

ing
rtable

EMBRACE YOUR WEIRDNESS

So, now you're at school there's a lot of work to do. But you're also going to make lots of friends and learn loads and loads about yourself too. When you arrive, you're relatively young and you have to rely on other people for many parts of your life, but you'll leave as a young adult, almost ready to drive a car, vote in elections and take your place in the world as a fully grown human person who's taking more and more responsibility for themselves. You'll look different, think differently – you'll be *You 2.0*, a more sophisticated, mature and knowledgeable version of the person reading this book right now.

This section of the book is all about how you can fit in while staying true to yourself on that journey to *You 2.0*. We'll talk about embracing your weirdness and all the things you love while wearing a uniform. We'll navigate making and breaking friendships. Then we'll explore what happens if you encounter a bully – or if you see someone being bullied.

But, before we start this bit, here's a little something that is actually true but people never admit to: everyone has, at some point in their lives, wished they were better at 'fitting in'. Yes, they wished that they had *those* trainers that **EVERYONE ELSE** in the year group has (they don't, just FYI). Or they wished they had gone to *that* thing on a

weekend in town that

everyone's going to but my stepdad won't let me

or that they'd been invited to that house party at *that* person's house that was, allegedly, **'SOOO GOOOD OHMYGODYOUSHOULD'VEBEENTHEREITWASTHEBEST NIGHTEVER.'**[1]

Fitting in isn't like a LEGO brick clicking into place or a door locking and then, hey presto, you're done! And that's truer than ever when you look online, where you might find yourself trying to be someone you think is a better version of you because their Instagram is full of sunsets and smiles. But how many times did the camera click for your friend to get that beach picture from last summer that got 456,743 likes?

[1] These parties aren't as dramatic or weird and wonderful as they sound. The reality is more likely that people will have had a good time and it will have been just … fine.

Plenty. Would it have had the same number (and would you have thought the same of it) if he or she had uploaded the one taken a second before that had a dog cocking its leg and peeing on the sand?

IT CAN BE EASY to wish you were more 'normal'.

If you were more like everyone else, you might think you would fit in better. You might also think that 'normal' people dress a certain way and appear to do what they should, when they should, acting in a way that society has decided people at this age, from this country, do. But never forget that everyone has those bits of themselves that they don't like; even the most apparently 'normal' person with the apparently 'perfect life' in your year will, I guarantee you, have times when they wish they were more like someone else.

More important than anything else,

you should be YOURSELF.

'Normal' is a clear, shiny paint people put on things to keep us feeling okay. It's the version of ourselves that gets shown to the outside world. Everyone's version of that is different. So if we let go of 'normal' being a thing, and realise that every single person is battling through some stuff, then we will start to realise that this person, you, reading this book – yes, **YOU** – is a brilliantly unique person. Let's do that, shall we? Good!

Every one of us – you, me, your mum, your dad, every single person in your maths class (which is as hard as reading a train timetable in Russian) – we all want to be liked, but remember that not every single one of us is going to be best friends with everyone else. Being the truest version of 'you', living your life and not trying to be someone else, is so important.

EMBRACE WHAT MAKES YOU UNIQUE

Life is what we make it. If we know that, then we'd better live life the way we want, hadn't we? The world is a big place, with so many colours, beliefs, haircuts, sights to see, people to meet, religions, achievements, styles of jeans, shoes, piercings, tattoos (not yet, mind – ask your folks when you turn 18 ...), places to live, sexualities, boxsets to watch, exams to pass, cars to drive, coffees to taste, people to fall in love with, people to fall out of love with, jobs to get, mountains to climb, romantic comedies to watch, dreams to dream, songs to sing and pictures to take. You'll meet people during the first few years of secondary school who you feel sure you *absolutely 100 per cent* will always be friends with. That will terrify your parents, though, in some cases – as maybe the friends you've made right now aren't the ones they'd have chosen for you, and they worry about the influence they might have. Sometimes it's someone they really worry about, and you just don't really understand why. That person might seem really quite lovely at that point in your life. And while that friend might be cool right about now, they might end up going from best friend, to friend, to acquaintance, to someone who 'likes' your posts online, to someone you end up muting on social media because they're doing your nut in. Friendships change and that's okay. They also *might* end up being your best friend until the end of time, and that's fine too!

Singer, songwriter, actress and author Dolly Parton said,

'FIND OUT WHO *YOU* ARE. AND DO IT ON PURPOSE.'

Dolly Parton –

American singer, songwriter, actress and author

Secondary school is a chance to do this and discover your possible place in the world. But it isn't about locking it down, clamping the cage shut and presenting the world with the final version of you. So if you feel something, let it out.

Be open. Be honest.

I guarantee you one huge thing – every single person reading this (and those not reading it, too) has made a mistake today. Everyone has also worried about something they wish they'd asked but didn't dare. Everyone has looked daft at some point in the last 24 hours to someone (and often it's to themselves). Think of this time of your life as going shopping for a new coat – you're going to go out and try a few on before you decide which one to buy. Even then, a coat's not for *ever* – it's for now!

So, embrace what makes you unique. If someone calls you a weirdo for wearing a lime-green and bright pink polka-dot hat to school, they might be right. But,

who actually cares?

It might be that you want your hair in a certain style; you want to be the centre of attention one day and not the next. You might love doing maths when your friends don't; you might like going to the stamp-collecting club after school but feel a bit embarrassed about it; you might not want to wear make-up to school; you might *want* to wear make-up. You could find trusting people hard or be unsure about your sexuality; you possibly like the idea of doing ballet in an after-school club; you could think you're the next Shakespeare and just *love* writing romantic poetry; you might have a fear of balloons² or find eye-contact difficult; you might like your trousers short or you might be that person who's really paranoid about a birthmark and worry about what people will say.

Whatever it is that makes you *you:*

Cherish it.

Try it on and see if it fits.

As long as you're not doing anything wrong, then you're doing right. Schools have rules (as do homes), so make sure you respect them, but schools and teachers are 100 per cent in favour of helping young people become empowered, strong and excellent in every way. Your learning about Shakespeare, Pythagoras and particles, and getting the best qualifications you can in those subjects is *really* important, and that will get your foot in the door of your dream job in a few years' time, but what gets you that dream job is the human being you are. Stand out. Be yourself.

Supermodel Alek Wek, who lived a really hard life before becoming one of the most famous models in the world, said,

---

² It's called globophobia. You're welcome. You learn something new every day!

'YOU ARE BEAUTIFUL. IT'S OKAY TO BE QUIRKY, IT'S FINE TO BE SHY. YOU DON'T HAVE TO GO WITH THE CROWD.'

Alek Wek -

South Sudanese-British supermodel

She's absolutely right – what makes you distinctive is what people know you for. So know it yourself, wear that coat and own it (until you see another coat that you think might be for you).

TRANSFORMING INTO A
SUPER
HERO:
YOUR UNIFORM

6

Now, here is the biggest challenge. As I've said, it's so important to be unique and not follow the crowd. But at the same time, there are rules, and one of the most annoying rules is that you have to wear a uniform. A uniform is really important, but one of the biggest things that can bother people in school is being told that they have to wear one.

I get it – it can be those stiff, starchy shirt collars, the tie ('Why do I have to wear a tie, sir? Nobody's getting married!'), the blazer, the trousers (especially after you've spent the entire summer holidays in joggers, shorts, jeans or a skirt). Some people wander into schools as if they're wearing a Tin Man costume – bulky, uncomfortable and dreadfully annoyed that someone else (usually the head teacher) is 'telling' them what they can wear. The regular complaint I hear about it is,

'But siiir, how does it affect my education?'

The truth is, it doesn't. A school uniform itself won't affect your education. Your black trousers *definitely* won't walk themselves into an exam at the end of the year and do a really good job. Your white shirt and bright yellow tie with a Latin motto and a picture of a creepy lion *absolutely* won't force your hand to pick up your pen to do the work on simultaneous equations in your last lesson on a Friday afternoon (when it's beautiful weather outside and your friends from the school down the road have a day off and are out on their bikes getting ice creams). Your black shoes *certainly* won't walk themselves down the corridor to your geography teacher's classroom to tell her that you've forgotten[1] your homework and save you an awkward conversation where she tells you she's 'more disappointed than annoyed'.

[1] Not done, let's be honest ...

DO WE REALLY HAVE TO WEAR IT?

So why do we have it? If Spider-Man's costume didn't protect him and help him shoot his web over villains, would he bother? If Black Widow didn't have the pistol holsters on her sides, what would be the point? Surely they'd both be better just wearing what they're comfortable in and they could do without the latex and leather?[2]

We all know that wouldn't be okay, don't we? If we think why, it's because Peter Parker *becomes* Spider-Man the second that costume goes on. While the person underneath technically stays the same, it's about the transformation from person at home to person at 'work'. Now, unless you're masquerading as a 12-year-old while actually being the CEO of a major international company, the likelihood is that your job, for now, is to be a student in your school.

The main reason you have to wear uniform is simply because it's the rules. And that might not seem like much of an answer, but there are actually great reasons to wear a uniform. If you

[2] I bet both are gross in summer. S-w-e-a-t-y. Eugh.

think about a police officer, a nurse or a fireman, they all have to put on a uniform when they go to work. It would be sort of odd if they wore their uniform all day long ... and it means that when they wear their uniform, they are in 'work' mode. When they're not, they're back to casual, normal life mode.

Putting on a uniform every morning gets you in the zone and makes you part of a team. And in the same way, a school uniform makes you switch into school mode. You're part of a school, which is bound together by certain things:

rules, expectations, lessons, corridors, classrooms and, yep, you guessed it: UNIFORMS.

Then, once you're home again, you can relax and wear whatever you want.

Everyone in a school is aiming for the same – and creating a sense of everyone being 'the same' is important. It's sort of saying 'out of school we might all be different but, between 9 a.m. and 4 p.m., we are all trying to do the same thing'. Everyone is wearing the same badge. Everyone shares responsibility for each other and *should* feel that sense of responsibility. There are other reasons, too. For people with huge walk-in wardrobes and 15 different clothing options for a mildly warm Wednesday in April, not having a uniform might be fine. They'll look great and have plenty of different things to wear the day after. They can, more than likely, look faaabulous all the time. They won't spend the night before constantly waking up and worrying about what they're going to wear because they don't have much. Plenty of people don't have that luxury, though. In fact, the *huge* majority of people don't have that luxury. What a uniform does is remove that worry –

we're all wearing the same.

There are no titters or laughs about the hole in that boy's shirt or the fact that she wore those jeans yesterday. While we're here, we're the same.

It's the same with piercings, tattoos[3] and all the rest of that jazz.

Whatever the rule is: FOLLOW IT.

No good comes from having a really painful nose piercing and then being told to take it out the following day. It sometimes ends up with home and school falling out, you being in the middle of it and then wishing you hadn't even bothered with it. What is definitely affected with stuff like piercings is your safety. Imagine rugby tackling someone, catching them just wrong and having a nose stud tear half your cheek off. In fact, think of drama, dance, food lessons, science experiments and the horrible consequences a slip and a nose piercing could cause. Eeek, not nice and not worth it ...

[3] AGAIN, DO NOT GET A TATTOO YET AS THEY ARE ILLEGAL UNTIL YOU ARE A FULLY GROWN HUMAN ADULT (18 YEARS OLD).

Teachers try their best to help everyone become a person who has everything that makes them happy, and that starts with everyone getting the same chances from the start. Looking across a sea of angelic terrified little faces at the start of the year with blazers the size of a wizard's cloak, it's clear everyone is at the same point. Having a really clear uniform creates 'uniform' (the same, yes?) expectations, and that helps us to get you where we want you to go.

So now that we've ditched the leather waistcoat and mustard-coloured flares that were in Paris Fashion Week, let's get on and work together, shall we? Errrm, excuse me – can we straighten that tie, please?

FRIENDSHIPS AND FALLOUTS

We've all watched TV and seen how secondary school is shown, especially on American programmes. Slow-motion smiles, happy tears and hugs at graduation; everyone laughing together and having fun in 'class'; corridor fun and games, even sometimes breaking into song;[1] and people skateboarding home to their massive houses with the sun always shining.[2] Well, if that's what you were expecting, you might need to think again.

The reality is that there'll be a huge percentage of your school life that, in ten years' time, will be like the faint ripples on the edge of a pool you threw a stone into half an hour ago. You'll barely even be able to remember it, and it probably wasn't *that* memorable anyway.

Primary school is the same. If you think back to Reception, do you remember *everything*? Probably not. Time cracks on quickly, and we have to make sure we get the best out of every moment.

Lots and lots of what we remember is not about *what* we do

---

[1] Actually, that's only *Annie* and *Glee*, from what I can remember ...
[2] And also, now I mention it, they all seem to have REALLY WHITE SMILES, don't wear uniform and have enormously expensive cars by the time they're just about past their final exams.

(you can't remember every picture you coloured in when you were four at pre-school ...) but *who* you did it with (... but you'll remember who some of those people you were colouring in with were). Some people come and stay, and some come and go. Secondary school can be a weird time for that, though – it can be like a friendship crossroads, where some tough decisions have to be made and some real blows can be felt.

MR BURTON'S TOP TIPS FOR MAKING A GOOD FIRST IMPRESSION AND MEETING PEOPLE LIKE YOU

1) Be you – people want honesty from their friends!
2) Don't be afraid to make conversation
3) Be nice – smile and look up!
4) Go to clubs that are to do with your interests – you'll bond with people there
5) Give it time – it takes time to make friendships!
6) Don't force it – some things are not meant to be!
7) Be comfortable – meet people where you'll both be comfortable and can properly chat
8) Use your lessons – if you're sitting next to someone, use it as a chance to chat (**BUT NOT WHEN THE TEACHER IS!**)

CLUBS AND SOCIETIES

There'll be loads and loads of new things you'll be doing in your lessons ... but also, there'll be lots more other things you can do that are extra to those lessons. For the first few weeks after your summer holidays you'll be tuning in to the new school and new school year (and probably be *so* tired after the holidays), so things will probably take a bit of time to get going. When the clubs start, though, choose one (at least), and

GO AND DO IT!

Whether it's sports, cookery, computer games, science, creative writing or debating, there'll be loads to choose from. They're such a good way to meet new people – people who like the things that *you do too*. And if there isn't a club or a society for the thing you love doing, talk to your teachers. I can't promise that they'll *definitely* be able to offer what it is that you want – after all, there are only so many teachers who can actually do recreating medieval battles with LEGO figurines. But they might be able to find something else that is similar and talk to you about your interests.

Other clubs might be linked to school work or doing homework, or they might just generally give you a chance to stick around in school for a while after it's finished. If there's a new baby crying the house down at home, or if you don't have a computer to do that piece of homework on, you might like to chill in the library for an hour, or you might want to ask your teachers for a few hints and tips. Teachers might have meetings sometimes, but they're usually always

HAPPY TO HELP!

NEW FRIENDS AND OLD FRIENDS

People often come to secondary school and stick with their friends from primary school like they've been sewn together and then glued just to make sure they definitely don't come apart. Nobody else exists. They don't want to know *anyone* from any other primary schools from down the road, round the corner, in the next town or anywhere.

NO, NO, NO.

A strange thing happens, though, as lessons start to get going. You meet other people. Different places, different cultures, different ways of doing things, different thoughts. And those people are interesting. In fact, these people could be potential new friends. This is exactly what secondary school is all about – meeting new people from different backgrounds and making friends!

But balancing new and old friendships can sometimes be confusing. That's because friendships are confusing, they're hard work and they take some time to get your head around. Sometimes they can feel like they make no sense, and you wonder why you even try! But they're so completely worth it. Stick at it – imagine you're in the canteen and this is going on right now. Stick with me; we'll act it out. Go and get a friend. I'll wait. No, go on. I'm waaaiting. Hurry up, it's Christmas soon … right, you're back. Here goes:

DAY 1 OF SECONDARY SCHOOL

It is lunchtime. Year 7 have had an excellent first morning, and Sam and Rozeena – best friends 4EVA LOL – are discussing their weekend plans over a tuna baguette.

> *Are you coming to my house this weekend like we said?* — **Sam**

> **Rozeena** | *Yeah, can I still stay over like your mum said?*

> *Think so. I'll ask. My mum will take us shopping in the afternoon and we'll get the bus home and get a pizza.* — **Sam**

> **Rozeena** | *Okay.*

> *What was your English lesson like? Who's that boy you're sat next to?* — **Sam**

> **Rozeena** | *It was good. Don't know who he is, he didn't talk, but I think his name is Jamal.*

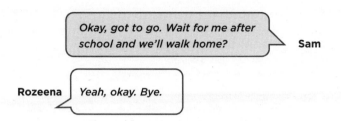

> Okay, got to go. Wait for me after school and we'll walk home? — **Sam**

> **Rozeena** | Yeah, okay. Bye.

Now these two are what is commonly known as bessies,[3] and right now neither think that will change. Why should it? Their mums are friends, their dads are friends; they have weekend plans and they don't need anyone else. They have other friends, and the whole group have been together since the first year of primary school. Lovely. But let's have a look at lunchtime a month later. Go get your friend again. Go on ...

DAY 35 OF SECONDARY SCHOOL

It is the final week before October half term. Rozeena is at Poetry Club, and Alex (she's new – another friend of theirs from primary school) is talking about it with Sam. Confusing, isn't it? That's friendships!

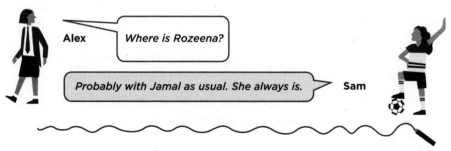

> **Alex** | Where is Rozeena?

> Probably with Jamal as usual. She always is. — **Sam**

[3] Meaning 'Best Friends' and not to be confused with 'Aunt Bessie's', the lady who makes frozen Yorkshire Puddings for supermarkets.

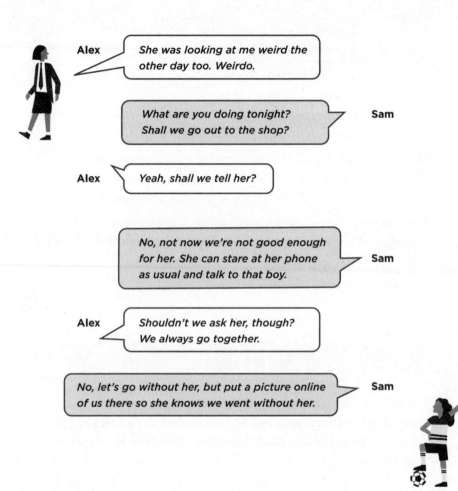

Alex: She was looking at me weird the other day too. Weirdo.

Sam: What are you doing tonight? Shall we go out to the shop?

Alex: Yeah, shall we tell her?

Sam: No, not now we're not good enough for her. She can stare at her phone as usual and talk to that boy.

Alex: Shouldn't we ask her, though? We always go together.

Sam: No, let's go without her, but put a picture online of us there so she knows we went without her.

Now, how does Rozeena feel? She's been excluded from something she didn't even know about with the people she's known for longer than anyone apart from her family. What's her crime? Going to a Poetry Club during lunchtime. Let's look at it from everyone's point of view, shall we?

✦ Sam

She feels like she's been pushed away from Rozeena's life because they were best friends, have been for ever and thought they always would be (they still can be, don't forget). She's hurt and upset because Rozeena seems to have some other friends and things that don't involve her, and she's feeling jealous of Rozeena's relationship with Jamal (who came from another school down the road). Sam's reaction is to try to make it look like she's having a good time without Rozeena, and make it obvious Rozeena's being excluded from plans with her group of friends. Sad face. ☹

✦ Rozeena

She's being excluded from her 'old' group of friends because she's making new friends. She feels torn between the people she already knows and the exciting world of secondary school with new people and new things to do outside of lessons. She *loves* writing poems so has gone to Poetry Club to work with her teacher. She loves her old friends just the same, but is really enjoying getting to know others, and Jamal is from a different part of town and is into the same music as she is. She's going to be sad when she sees that plans have been made without her, and she will wish she hadn't seen it.

✦ Alex

She doesn't quite know what to do. She likes poetry too, but has seen how Sam reacts when people don't do what she expects. She'll go along to the shop tonight but will send Rozeena a message so she knows that it wasn't her idea. She feels weird and doesn't like how things are between them all.

So what will happen, and how can it be saved? Well, the main thing that will help is that important word 'communication'. If Sam understands that Rozeena still cares for her but is just embracing the new opportunities in school, then she might feel better. It's hard being on the outside and, unfortunately, everyone here feels like they're outside, fighting for a way back in. It might be that over the next few months and years the whole group slowly drifts apart, and that growing up, growing older and having different things to be interested in naturally means they slowly become acquaintances[4] rather than friends. But it also might be that that doesn't happen, and things are defused because of a moment when they see each other in the corridor, away from other people, and just have a chat, talking about how they feel. Nobody can definitely say what will happen with friendships – you can't force them! But good friendships are worth working at and communication is the key.

---

[4] People you'd say 'hi' to in a corridor, rather than high five, fist bump, hug or perform a really elaborate handshake with that takes 20 minutes to complete. A diluted friend.

GOSSIP

Sometimes friendships can get complicated because when someone feels they've been let down by someone else (for example Sam), they think one of the easiest ways to 'get back' at someone is by spreading a story, a rumour or gossip about them. It could be a friend, someone who's definitely *not* a friend, or it could even be a teacher, and it happens every day. This stuff isn't new – it was around in the Victorian times when I was at school, too – but it's changed recently, as social media, the internet and mobile phones have become a bigger part of what we do every day. And if you don't have a mobile phone or social media just yet, the likelihood is that you will do over the next few years. Being a teenager (or nearly a teenager) is hard. I can say 'ignore it' until I'm blue in the face, but when people are saying nasty things about you, sending pictures of you (which is *not* allowed at *all*) or are being unkind (and we know about the importance of kindness, don't we?), it's easy to crumble. The more difficult rumours for you to deal with are those that *could* be true or, in some cases, *are* true. They could be something you told someone who has slipped up and blurted it out, or they could be completely false, but whatever the rumour is, get this:

it isn't nice to go through.

Gossip can spread quickly. If we say that someone will tell five people within ten minutes, and then each of those five people tell a few more within a few minutes, then that would be bad enough, but it doesn't stop there. The phones come out and gossip can spread like wildfire – then someone from the school down the road somehow gets involved and it turns into a really big, stinking mess of a situation, and everyone who was there to start with feels dreadful about it. If it happens, open up and talk. If you get any of these messages about someone, think about how *you* would feel. Don't ever forget what costs nothing and can make every single human being's life just that little bit better every day:

kindness.

FRIENDS FOR LIFE

Use that bouncebackability that we've talked about before in these sorts of situations. Friendships are tough to navigate and keep, and just because you have known each other for ever and ever, it doesn't mean it's always going to be that way. You'll make lots of new friends as you progress through life and that's important.

Friends are GREAT.

They can help you with your homework, support you when you're feeling down, make you laugh-out-loud when you're sitting in science and the teacher does that funny thing no one else has noticed ... and whatever your squad looks like at the end of school is a true reflection of you, what you like doing, wearing, listening to and playing at that point in your life. When you move to college, it'll change; when you get a job, it'll change again. It'll keep evolving and changing, and that's part of the beauty of being a human being!

'WALK AWAY FROM FRIENDSHIPS THAT MAKE YOU FEEL SMALL AND INSECURE, AND SEEK OUT PEOPLE WHO INSPIRE YOU AND SUPPORT YOU.'

Michelle Obama – *American lawyer, author, activist and former First Lady of the United States*

So, enjoy your friends, but

live your own life and do what makes *you* wear a smile.

Enjoy being with people who make you happy, and if you find yourself on the outside, looking into a group, then think about whether that group is actually what you want. If it is, and you've made a mistake and could apologise for something, then do what's right. If they're being unkind (remember – being kind is *so* important), then there are plenty of others. Find people who are your type of people, who treat you right and who respect you for being the person you are.

Why?

Because you're brilliant, and you deserve to be respected.

BULLYING:
THE HARD
TRUTH

Bullying is horrible. There's no other way to describe it. You can't dress it up, put make-up and lipstick on it and make it have a lovely accent so it looks or sounds better.

It's horrible.
Horrible.
Horrible.
Horrible.

I'm glad we've got that sorted before we go any further.

There won't be any part of this that starts to even say it isn't, or that it's in people's heads, or that it's made up, because it's not. Whatever you feel, you feel, and if someone is making you feel that way on purpose, then that's bullying.

I also won't sit here writing this and pretend that it isn't going to happen to anyone in any school anywhere, and I certainly won't say that just because you've read this chapter of this book that it somehow makes you immune from someone making you feel like rubbish. Schools can punish people who are bullying others, and can do a brilliant job of helping anyone who has been, or is being, bullied, but they absolutely can't 100 per cent completely and utterly and without a single question *stop* it from happening. It's been around since the start of time, and it will (unfortunately) be around until schools stop being schools and education is downloaded from a memory stick into your head and we live in space or something.[1]

Rubbish, really, isn't it?

I can't give you a single killer line that would floor any bully in this chapter, but I can give you a few things that, I think, are the best ways of coping if it happens. Because if it does happen, then the best thing to do is get it dealt with quickly so that it stops, and do whatever you can to make sure it doesn't happen again.

[1] Which is a very jazzy way of saying 'never'. Unfortunately.

MY EXPERIENCE OF THE BULLIES

I was bullied. It was awful. I didn't say anything for ages, and I thought it was all my fault. I felt like I must have done something to deserve it, and I also thought it would be really embarrassing to say anything at all about it – I didn't want my mum and dad to worry about me, and I assumed my teachers were too busy. It all started after a French lesson, and my 'crime' was not to have a rubber this chap could borrow. I didn't have a rubber – what could I have done about that?! I suppose I could have popped to the shops during lunchtime and refreshed the contents of my pencil case, but I never thought of that.[2] After that lesson, he pushed me down some stairs as we all went back into school.

From then on, he would tell everyone he was going to 'get' me at any point he could. I was a 'geek'[3] – and I was terrified. On the outside, I pretended it didn't bother me at all – I 'styled it out'[4] and made a joke of it. Inside, though, it worried me. It was like a little mouse gnawing away in my

---

[2] Funny, that, as a boy of 14.
[3] Cool now, not so much then. Basically it means I did my homework, went to all my lessons and didn't do anything wrong.
[4] As much as you can be stylish about something when your favourite coat is a bright red Disney fleeced jacket.

mind, constantly there and worrying me. Even when it was the evening or weekend, doing my favourite things, I couldn't ever really relax or properly enjoy it. I just sort of accepted that this was how things were now, and that it would stay like that until one of three things happened: he left school, I left school or school finished.

It went on like this for ages. It was summer term – the days were hot and everyone was outside all the time at break and lunch. He would stare, whisper to his friends while looking at me and release threats at regular intervals that would reach me fifth hand about the damage he was considering doing to my head/legs/house/parents (mainly my mum).[5] I'd make my way inside and find a corner in which to spend the last ten minutes of break, and then when it came time to make my way to my lesson, I'd avoid the areas where I knew he'd be – even if it meant my route became a 49-hour trip via Hong Kong and New Zealand.

Then the day came when he went for me. Tuesday afternoon, after maths, in June. I knew something was up when I left the lesson (I always darted my eyes around to see whether he was around before I set off walking anyway), and on this occasion I saw him. My heart stopped and I just knew what was about to happen.

Long story short, he messily bundled me into a corner (he was much bigger than me) and rained punches down on my

[5] Everyone always goes for the mums, don't they? Classy.

head. Most of them missed, and the only ones that really connected hit my body, so my spotty face wasn't made even less beautiful as a result. Phew!

I left school and had to go to an interview for my work experience placement just after that. I jumped on the bus into town, and I can still remember the feeling of being utterly, completely and absolutely alone. Weird, because I had a load of friends and a brilliant family, but holding on to this single experience myself was just

... isolating.

Something had to be done – and I told myself that I wouldn't let this chap control my life for any longer. Plotting his demise was going to go one of two ways: I could either stake out his movements, find out where he lived and order 300 pizza deliveries per day to his house, all addressed to 'Mr Bully', or I could, and probably far more easily and legally, tell someone.

Telling someone wasn't a laugh a minute, though. It wasn't easy. While the words I actually *said* were along the lines of 'this boy is bullying me and it's making me really sad', in my own mind, I actually heard myself say, 'I've lost control and I'm really weak and I don't know what to do so I'm running to my form tutor for help.' As I've grown up and got older, I've realised that I wasn't saying that at all – I was doing what I should have done weeks ago. My form teacher disappeared, sorted it, and that was that.

Relief.

Except it wasn't the end of it. Whenever I saw him in a corridor, it still bothered me. It was still in the back of my mind that he'd surely have more of a reason to thwack me on the back of the head or pile-drive me into a locker like some Road Runner cartoon. It didn't happen, but that doesn't mean that the effect just magically disappeared the moment my (brilliant) form teacher 'handled it' for me.

I'm not writing this so that you pull out a violin and play some sad music while my eyes go all teary as if I've been cutting a thousand onions for an assault on the Guinness World Record for the 'World's Biggest Bowl of Onions'.[6] But I do want you to take something away from this chapter, because I'll be honest about what I did, what I wish I'd done and what I know now, being on the 'other side' of it.

So, if you take something away, fantastic (and hopefully not just a faint smell of onions from imagining the thing

---

[6] My ultimate goal.

above), and if you're not going through it right now but think you might be the guy or gal making someone feel like this (whether you actually mean it or not), then take a bit of time to mull it over and remember that we're all human beings – nobody is born *asking* to be picked on. Experiencing bullying is tough. But you can and you will get through it – and there will be people there to support you.

'HOWEVER DIFFICULT LIFE MAY SEEM, THERE IS ALWAYS SOMETHING YOU CAN DO AND SUCCEED AT.'

Professor Stephen Hawking –
English physicist, cosmologist and author

MR BURTON'S TIPS FOR WHAT TO DO IF YOU THINK YOU'RE BEING BULLIED

⭐ 1) It happens to us all

At some point in your school life, it's highly likely that someone's going to do or say something that makes you feel rubbish. It'll hurt, and it'll make you sad. It could be your mortal enemy from the mean streets of Tunbridge Wells who once knocked you off your scooter when you were seven, or it could be your friend. Either way, let's be real about it: at some point, however light and small it might be, someone's going to do something to you that they have chosen to do, and that thing will upset you. That doesn't mean it's okay, and it's not a reflection on you. You're worthy of being treated with respect; always remind yourself of that.

⭐ 2) Don't bottle it up

I stood for it. I didn't tell anyone. How I wish I hadn't just taken it now. It ruined the 1998 World Cup in France for me[7]

---

[7] Michael Owen, that wondergoal against Argentina; Sol Campbell's (wrongly) disallowed goal in extra time; and David Batty's penalty that saw us knocked out. Again.

(I didn't go; I just watched it on telly). When England were playing, I had half a mind on the bullying. Four years of waiting for an international football tournament ... and then it's ruined by a mindless thug with a grudge. The minute I spoke up it started to get better. Adults (and friends) are around you to support and help you; they won't belittle you or say you're lying or suggest you're to blame. They're your team, your gang, your people. Trust in them. Honestly – tell someone, and it'll start opening the door to let help in. The old saying is 'a problem shared is a problem halved', and you don't how true it is until you share a problem and it splits like a Chocolate Orange. Even if those around you aren't the people you need to talk to, there are online and phone services you can call for help and advice – all free and completely confidential. (I've listed some resources on page 204.) Just, please, talk about it. People want to know.

✫ 3) All bullying comes from somewhere

We all like to think of bullies as being 'different' to us – we'd never do anything like that to anyone, would we? Surely you're not suggesting that I would go out of my way to intentionally hurt someone or cause them upset? Well, sadly, the realistic situation is that, just as we've all been bullied at some point, most of us have actually been bullies at some point, too. Whether you're stressed out about school, you're worrying about something at home, your dog's not very well or you lost a game of FIFA last night and now you have to perform some sort of embarrassing, humiliating forfeit for it; all and any of these can make us feel like someone deserves to feel the sadness we're feeling too. We sometimes lash out at those closest to us – best mates and family – and that can lead to us making someone feel dreadful even if we never ever intended to make them feel that way. Once that happens, it can happen again and again and again, so a huge chain of misery is caused.

If you're doing this stuff, you can stop. There are so many reasons why, but I'll pick on just one: how would you feel if that person you're making feel like that was you or someone you love? People can help, and they want to help and put a stop to this stuff, so, again, just ask. Have a think about what is making you act in this way and try to get to the bottom of it. Make a difference today, and you can change someone's life with a click of your fingers. Not only theirs, but your own. Go on – I know it's hard, but you can do it.

⭐ 4) Recognise the signs

Online

A lot of bullying nowadays starts online. Probably from a comment about something that wasn't supposed to be taken in a certain way, or by two people talking then one of them sending a screenshot of that chat to someone else. The 'why' can be really hard to pin down, but the 'what' can be awful. Threatening messages, nasty language and threats to turn it physical when they see you are all really common. If it happens, most social media sites have a button to report it, and you should also block the person who's giving you a hard time. If it doesn't have a button to report, it's not a site you should be using ... so keep safe.

Physical

Punching, kicking, hitting, grabbing and generally being violent and nasty, or touching you in a way that you really don't like. Often this is done quietly, where the bully thinks people can't see – but you can feel it. It's hard not to react in a certain way sometimes, but keep yourself safe, report it and know that you don't have to accept someone treating you in that way.

Psychological

Names, 'jokes' (that are about you) and threats are really common for this. It could be someone close to you, who's in your friendship group and is taking it out on you because they're not happy about something. It can make you feel tiny and pointless and not want to come to school and

THAT IS NOT OK!

⭐ 5) Continue to be aware

It doesn't always just stop dead. I was lucky and it *sort of* did. So don't rest until it's actually sorted. Not sorted and swept away so it's 'dealt with', but *actually stopped* because that person is no longer doing it. Do you feel better? If not, it's not good enough. Keep asking the questions until you are.

And finally, a note to you: if you're in the middle of this, I'm really sorry. It isn't somewhere anyone wants to be, and you might not be able to see a way out. There is one, though – you just need to take that first step and talk to someone. And that could be *anyone*. It could be the person you would expect to go to – your form tutor or head of year – and they're probably the staff member who most would go to. But there are plenty of other people you *could* speak to – everyone in school is trained to deal with things like bullying, so go to whoever you're most comfortable talking to, let them know what's going on and they'll do something about it. It could be the head teacher, someone in the office, exams officer, receptionist, physics teacher or the technology technician. They'll be really glad that you trusted them enough to talk to them about it. Never lose faith that good people can help. That moment when you finally tell someone will be a huge turning point for you: just do it! They'll help. You might not feel like you're enough, but you *are*, and don't let anyone tell you differently. You don't deserve this, and there is a way out.

WHAT TO DO IF YOU SEE SOMEONE BEING BULLIED

If you think others are being bullied and you can see it, then do something. Don't be a superhero and destroy whole cities to protect your friend from someone pulling them a dirty look, but do *something*.

The easiest thing to do if you see someone getting bullied is to pretend you didn't see. If the bully is a bigger person, is well known as being 'hard', then I get it. I understand why you'd want to pop it to one side and go about your day.

But how would that make you feel?

Honestly, I think you'd feel pretty rubbish about yourself. Now, there's no part here where I'm going to tell you to run from one end of the maths corridor to the other and absolutely wipe out the bully with a massive whack. That is 100 per cent definitely, without any question, *not* the way to deal with this. I also *really* don't want you to loudly bring attention to it by organising a group of others in your year (or the years above you) to 'get' him or her on the way home. These have all been done in the history of bullying and have never, ever worked. These are definitely *not* the way to deal with situations that need a little more time and care. What happens when you pour more petrol on a fire?[8] Yep, it spits out more flames – it becomes even more hot and more dangerous than it was before.

You can't solve the world's problems all by yourself, and to help the person being bullied you have to understand that you, alone, can't stop it. But you can do a couple of things. These little somethings might not sound all that glamorous, and certainly not as epic as mounting the equivalent of a police SWAT team on your mountain bikes and performing a citizen's arrest in the middle of town on Saturday afternoon in front of his or her mummy, but they are effective.

✷ 1) Firstly, put yourself in their shoes[9]

Think about what being bullied must be like. It's awful.

---

[8] If you don't know, DO NOT TRY AND FIND OUT!
[9] Don't steal their shoes – that's not what I mean! They've got enough problems without walking home with no shoes!

Being pushed and pulled and spoken about and laughed at and being the butt of everyone's jokes is horrible.

How would you feel?

✭ 2) Have a little word in their ear

No, you're not a trained counsellor or doctor, and you certainly can't make it go away, but you can let them know that someone's going to be there for them. A simple hello, a friendly smile or sitting next to them at lunch can honestly make someone's day. If they're expecting the world to be against them, you could be that someone who just proves to them that there is good out there ... and it's worth

keeping positive.

✭ 3) Tell someone who can do something

As I've said, taking the law into your own hands and saying, 'I'll sort this ...' may seem the easiest way to stop it happening, but it will not end well. Don't get involved physically, even if your arms are like massive pythons and you can lift three double-decker buses with one finger.

The smart way to support the victim is to pass it on and tell someone responsible. Just make sure that someone *older* knows.

They can, and will, do something about it, and they can, and will, make sure it

STOPS without any more hurt, harm, or heads being butted.

So, if you're sitting in a lesson right now and you've just seen that happen – a trip in the corridor, a push in the back, a picture that's been sent around or anything else you wouldn't want to happen to *you* – then you have a duty. Firstly, put this book down, as I'm pretty sure you shouldn't be reading it in a lesson, and then secondly, tell someone. Nobody wants anyone to feel like they're worthless, and you can help right now.

Go on, do your bit ...

LIVING
IN THE
SPOTLIGHT

I grew up in what seems like the 1800s,[1] and back then a phone was something you had in your house – and only one per household.[2] Mobile phones were the sort of things that only REALLY IMPORTANT PEOPLE who did BUSINESS had, and they were usually called car phones. They were basically like a brick from the side of your house in black plastic (and they weighed about the same, too), with a breadstick for an aerial. It cost about £30 a minute to talk to anyone, and they were pretty useless. Nobody had one. They were like unicorns – people talked about them, but nobody actually thought they existed.

And then, all of a sudden, the internet arrived and mobile phones moved out of cars. And then people started texting.[3] And then Myspace and Bebo and eventually Facebook popped up. And then they evolved into mobile phone apps, and others came along, and here we are today, where you can, with a single click, tell someone exactly where you are, who you're with, what you're eating, what you think of it, and

[1] But actually it was in the 1990s, only a few years ago.
[2] At a stretch, you might have three: one in your kitchen, one in the lounge and one in your parents' bedroom that were all connected so you could quietly pick one up and listen to your brother's conversations on the other – oh, the FUN we had …
[3] But only in 160 characters, leading to stuff like 'R U GONNA COME 2NITE IT WILL BE FUN LOL', almost single-handedly destroying the English language overnight.

provide a picture to prove it (because did you even have a Starbucks if you didn't get it on the internet and use the word 'cheeky' to describe it?).

You might not have a mobile phone just yet but, at secondary school, the pressure to be online, splattered across social media and chucking out daily selfies with eyebrows 'on point' is likely going to grow and grow and grow. The world exists with this great parallel reality, where you will interact with people at school over the internet and yet they won't even blink at you in the corridor. That's fine, sometimes, and people are allowed to enjoy finding out new things, meeting new people and having chats with them, but it's really important to be safe. While that's not exactly the world's most fashionable word, and you'll have sat through plenty of assemblies and lessons about online safety, it is *so* important. Homework responsibilities don't stop the day you get a phone and a Snapchat account, and just because you got 297 likes on a picture of you in front of a sunset on holiday that your dad had to take 76 times with the caption 'Living my best life ...', it doesn't mean you can now call yourself an 'influencer'.

WITH GREAT POWER COMES GREAT RESPONSIBILITY

Unfortunately, homework and phones are not best friends.[4] The benefits of helping the learning you've done at school sink into your brain by doing a homework task are *huge*, but even if you're dreading doing it, are tired and it has to be done in the next 12 hours, don't try to do it with your phone in your hand. Every time it pings you'll be over to it.

Put it away.
Turn it off.

Do whatever you need to, and separate the two: homework and screen time.

---

[4] In fact, they fell out over an incident involving a stolen piece of brown toast and don't speak at all now.

And what good comes from having phones in schools *anyway*? We've already talked about bullying, and phones can play a major part in it. It can take seconds to say something nasty on a phone (and it's certainly easier than saying it to someone's face), but it is *never* a good idea to bully people online. It leaves the person who's doing it in real trouble, and it also feels awful to be picked on and see it spread widely across all your friends (and other people who aren't your friends, too). You might be mad at someone, but there are better ways to talk about it than start a huge argument over social media. As you and the person you've had a go at get more and more hurt and upset (because this doesn't stop when school finishes), everyone else in your year sits with popcorn watching it play out over the internet.

Not a good look, and not good to have to deal with the day after!

So, with great power comes great responsibility (said Spider-Man's uncle, once upon a time), and let me tell you a secret that many teachers don't want you to know:[5] many of you lot are better at phones than many of your teachers. We'll always try to get ahead of the game, but by the time we've downloaded Snapchat or Facebook or Instagram, it's usually about the same point that your mum and dad have done the same and it's become a little bit ... you know ... meh. So teachers are a bit behind on this stuff, usually, which means it's *really, really, really* important that when you are online independently, you make good decisions. Nobody can get in your skin and actually decide to press a certain button, or click a certain link, or take a particular picture apart from you, but there are a few golden rules to live by when you're setting sail in the great social media ocean. It can get a little bit rough, so it's *really* important that you protect yourself as much as you can.

[5] Please don't tell anyone, because I'll get into trouble.

TOP TIPS FOR SURVIVING ONLINE

⭐ 1) Don't write anything that you wouldn't wear on a T-shirt on Saturday afternoon in the shopping centre

I know it might feel like it, but having a conversation online is *not* like having a chinwag over a cup of tea at your nan's house. What you say to her will only go as far as her friend Brenda when they go to the luncheon club (and Brenda can't even hear any more and is far more interested in listening to the bingo anyway). You can talk to some people in your life with the confidence that those words will go no further. There'll be people in your life that you'll hurt with your words but who will bounce back and love you regardless because you're you, you said it to them, and they know you said it because you were tired, angry, sad, poorly, just a bit off it or for any other reason.

Talking online doesn't have these benefits. Anything you say can be grabbed, photographed, downloaded, saved to camera roll and sent on to thousands of people. These people aren't your nan, they aren't your family, and won't be interested in whether you were tired, angry, sad, poorly, just a bit off it or any other reason when you sent it.

The simple way to do things is to live by this rule: if you wouldn't write the message you're about to send to that person in your year on a T-shirt and go into the local shopping centre wearing it, then don't send it. If you wouldn't want that selfie you're going to send to someone to be printed on scatter cushions and spread across the sofa in your living room when everyone comes round on a Sunday afternoon, then

don't send it.

If you wouldn't say that comment on a link you're about to make to the same person if you were introduced to them tomorrow, then

Look after yourself and think about what your actions say about you. Are you proud of that person who's the 'online' you? If so, then brilliant. If not, maybe it's time to make a change.

✦ 2) Talk

It's very, very easy to end up feeling like you can't get out of a problem when you're stuck in it. Let's get one thing straight, though: if you've messed up, it can (usually) be fixed. The internet is an adult's playground, handed to young people – like jumping from pre-school to graduation in one jump – and it can be a really terrifying place. You will make mistakes, you will click on the odd thing that you shouldn't, and you might end up seeing something you really wish you hadn't. While you can't always stop that, what you can do is open up and tell someone about it. Every single day I see amazing young people who want to deal with their own business, and that's great, but asking questions, seeing whether things are quite right, and letting people know if you're not happy is really important.

And what's more, these people *want to help*. How good is *that?* Right now, you have a fantastic forcefield of amazing humans around you who will fight your battles, support you with everything you do and want to know when things are good or bad. You might get sent a message or be asked to send someone a picture, or get a friend request from someone that just makes you think that something's not quite right. *Please* tell someone. Without knowing, we can't help, and by *goodness*, we want to. Not to shout and bawl at you, tell you off or judge you – that's not important – but because we care about you and want you to be happy.

Talk to friends, too. What people share can make their life look **AM-A-ZING**, but there might be something they're hiding, scared of or worried about. If they've been up until 4 a.m. posting stuff that worries you, you need to pass that on. It's likely that they're fine, but it's not a risk you should be willing to take. Talk to someone or report it on the website they were on. Look out for the people around you and don't assume that all those happy, smiling photos they posted days before aren't covering up how sad they might be feeling in real life.

Finally, make sure you have a good chat with your parents or guardians about what you're up to. There are apps they can use to track your usage, location and all sorts of wonderful things, which you can work out between you. While you might not want to let them to start with, some of these things might come in really useful and help you out.

Oh, and if you find any funny YouTube videos of hamsters playing pianos, pass 'em on too, yeah?[6]

⭐ 3) Sleep

Have you ever been in a car that has run out of petrol and just bumps to a stop? Have you ever got in the shower and realised too late that it's *freezing* and there's no hot water? Have you ever got ready to play football with your pals before noticing nobody's brought a ball? Have you ever tried to bake a cake before realising you haven't got any flour?

---

[6] Or anything else hilarious, for that matter …

If important ingredients are missing, things don't work. The car stops without fuel. The shower is cold because there's no gas. The game can't start without a ball. The cake is pretty disgusting and is basically just a sugary-eggy mess.

You're the same. You don't work right without key ingredients, and one of the most important ones of those is

Now, I know it's really tempting to have 'one last game on FIFA' or keep saying 'No, *you* hang up' to your new love interest, but **PLEASE PUT THE PHONE DOWN OR YOU WILL BE A WRECK TOMORROW**. Mobile phones, some TVs and computers give out 'blue light', which can have a *massively bad* impact on how you sleep. It can stop your body producing something called melatonin – also known as the vampire hormone, as it only comes out at night – which helps you get to sleep. It is definitely **NOT** going to make you attractive to bats and help you to inherit a large Romanian castle, but it will help you to sleep, to feel fantastic, and to get yourself into the school zone.

Put your phone somewhere it can't bother you at night. You need to be at your best the day after, so rather than drag yourself, knackered, through geography tomorrow, give yourself a time when it goes down and stays down (and not 3 a.m.).

⤝ 4) Smell a rose

The world is brilliant. People are amazing. Friends are lovely. Cuddles are warm. Flowers smell stonking[7] (but horses don't). Sunsets are beautiful. Rain smells incredible.

All these things don't need to be shared online. Enjoy your life without being strung up like Pinocchio and led by a piece of technology in your hand.

That sunset did happen, even if it's not on Instagram. Your friend did make you feel lovely by saying 'I like your jeans' without you needing to share a picture of them online, and you do feel just so amazing having run home in the rain from school without needing to map it on a running tracker and then sharing it with the entire world.

Enjoy your life.

[7] Actually, I'm not convinced they do. I've always been told that they do. People (mainly mums) smell them and say, 'Oooh, they're beautiful.' I've always thought they smell like fresh air and hay fever. Is that just me? Can I get a 'HELL YEAH'? Oh, it is just me. Ignore me, then.

Put the phone down and revel in the fact that you are alive, and you are loved.

⭐ 5) Don't dive in

Please don't assume that I think this stuff is really, really simple. I know it isn't. Loads of people are tempted to do the easiest thing possible to become popular when they start at school. The most difficult thing, sometimes, is to do the *right* thing. Mobile phones can do loads of good for you in school – they can let you see the inside of a classroom and connect with other people in your year group on the other side of the world, and they can give you any piece of information you could ever need for any piece of homework you could ever get within seconds – but they can also do a lot of bad. People record fights and spread them across social media; people do and say daft things to others online that they wouldn't in the real world to appear popular, forgetting that they have to do an experiment on osmosis with them in science the day after.

You're a young person, and you *are* allowed to make mistakes.

They're part of growing up.

In fact, mistakes on phones and online are a part of growing up, too. But just remember, when something doesn't quite feel right, it usually isn't right, and if your 'Spider sense' tingles – remember, great power and great responsibility – then say no, and don't dive in.

Mobile phones, the internet and everything that revolves around them have such power to do good, but also such power to make people feel awful. So maybe give yourself a break from them and leave them at home once in a while.

Just be kind, be sensible and talk – that's all anyone will ever ask you to do.

Conqu
Chall

ering

enges

BUT I'M NOT VERY GOOD AT THAT ...

What's your favourite subject at school? Write it down. Now, write the reasons why you've chosen it too. Without seeing what you've written (and I can't, of course, as this book doesn't have hidden cameras to spy on what you've written),[1] I reckon your reasons might include a few of the following things:

- I like the teacher
- I'm good at it
- I've always done well in it
- It's interesting
- My mum helps me with it
- I've had to work hard at it and now I can do it
- I'm proud of my work in it
- It's good[2]
- Don't know[3]

Often, we like things we can do well. I always *loved* English. Why? Because I could do it. I felt safe and secure, like I wouldn't get a lot wrong, and that whatever I was given to do,

[1] Or *does* it? That's what a book without hidden cameras would say, of course ...
[2] If that's one of them, that's *rubbish* – you can do better ...
[3] That's even *worse*!

I would be able to do quite a good job of it. I felt confident and, probably because of those things (and the fact that they said I was really good at it), I really liked my teachers.

Easy.
Job done.
School - complete.

But it's not, though, is it? Everyone's got something they're good at, that they could do with their eyes closed,[4] but a mahoosive[5] part of secondary school is about putting the hard work in with those subjects where all you can think is, **OHMYGOODNESSMETHISISSOHARD!** Not a fan of simultaneous equations? You're going to need to know them! Can't manage to bend your mind around Shakespeare[6] and why Macbeth was hanging around with witches on the moor? It needs to go into your head somehow.

[4] Unless it's javelin throwing in PE or chopping something up in Food Technology – DO NOT DO THAT WITH YOUR EYES CLOSED!
[5] Massive, but even more massive.
[6] I was going to put 'Can't shake a spear at Shakespeare?' but then realised that sounded STOOPID and made absolutely no sense. Just so you know ...

So, how do we make it through those tough moments in the lessons you enjoy the least when it's hot – you feel like the classroom is some kind of greenhouse which is melting you alive in your blazer and tie, and all you want to do is stare out of the window or shout, **'AAARGHHH! THIS IS RAAABBISH!'** – and actually take what we need and learn from those moments? Well, there is no shortcut, I'm afraid. In my experience it comes down to a few tips, but one big thing: work hard. Get grafting.

The connections you make and the questions you ask in those subjects are more important than any others. If your starting point in the subjects you don't like is behind where it is in your favourite subjects, then you'll have to try even harder to make more progress and get where you're going. You can either look at that as something to be afraid of (don't) or something to challenge yourself with. The brilliant thing about starting your new school, though, is that it is a whole new world,[7] and what you used to think was a subject you weren't good at (or didn't like) might, with a new perspective, seem very, very different. So, here are my tips for working through those subjects you see on your timetable and think, *Oh no, not again*. Turn those frowns upside down and make those subjects your best friends ...

[7] Not in an *Aladdin* way. I don't know of *any* secondary schools that have flying carpets and lamps with genies in (unless you count teachers as genies).

✮ 1) Let go of the past

You might not think you have a lot of love for something at school because of a load of reasons: you could have had a false start and been away the first time something was taught, you might have missed some of the important ideas behind what you're supposed to do.

This is a chance to change that!

Give all of that up, and

GO FOR IT!

Sometimes with a bit of 'newness' we end up loving the things we really don't expect to enjoy!

✮ 2) What do you know?

Write down what you know about the subject **RIGHT NOW**, maybe before you even step into a classroom. I bet you'll surprise yourself with what you do actually remember. There'll be something useful in your head about it, for sure! Feel confident – you know that, now what's next?

⭐ 3) What don't you know?

This is probably in the driving seat of why you don't like a subject. What is it that you feel you should know that you don't? Not just maths or science or French, but what specifically about those subjects? Where did you feel like you lost yourself in the Forest of Maths, leaving you cold, alone and with the light quickly fading? Let's try to pick a path back and see what it is that you *don't* know, and then, with your teacher's help, you'll be able to identify the one or two bits that can allow you to find the right path again. Imagine you're a mechanic – you need to get 'under the bonnet' of that subject and find out what's wrong. You wouldn't go interfering with a car's engine if you didn't have an idea about what to do with certain bits, would you? You'd want to get your head around what's going on. It's the same for subjects – understand what is being asked of you and what you need to do, and then you have a better chance of succeeding (and enjoying it along the way)!

⭐ 4) What's the big picture?

Why are you doing this subject? For example, in my English classroom, I've heard plenty (millions)[8] of people claim

[8] Maybe not *quite* millions, but definitely over ten.

they'll 'never need Shakespeare again', so 'why do I have to do it?' Well, there are a load of answers, but the main one is **BECAUSE HE IS THE MOST FAMOUS PLAYWRIGHT IN ENGLISH HISTORY AND IS BRILLIANT!**[9] Your teachers are trying to inspire you, and are playing their part in getting you ready for the big wide world. That *definitely* doesn't mean the big picture is to do **EXAM, EXAM, EXAM** for **YEARS**, but what you cover early in your subjects (including those that you don't feel the love for), you'll need in the future.

Another subject that can be really divisive is PE or 'games' (as it used to get called millions of years ago when I was at secondary and we used to ride dinosaurs to school instead of getting the bus). Some people love it and are the best at everything. They're the captain of every team going – football, netball, rugby, cricket, swimming; you name it, they're the captain of the team – and just awesome at anything involving physical exercise. Some people aren't, though, and can't even stomach the thought of getting changed in front of other people and actually standing on a cold field getting muddy. It can make you feel awkward, self-conscious and paranoid. Most people starting out at secondary school, though, probably fall between the two extremes. But sport is important. In fact, exercise is a *really* important part of life; it keeps us fit, it can help keep us happy and give us a lift

---

[9] Shakespeare also invented SO MANY of the words we use these days, too. Ever heard of a footballer *elbowing* someone – '… and the defender elbows the striker straight in the face and his nose looks like a squashed fruit'? He made that up. Ever felt *lonely* and put some sad music on and had a cry? Then you've used his word. Has anyone ever accused you of *silliness*? No, I'm sure they haven't either, but that's ANOTHER Shakespeare classic.

when we're not quite at our best. A lot of people spend time in sporting clubs outside of school – but for almost everyone, the *definite* chance you'll have to do some exercise (and so help keep you fit) will be in PE. If something about it bothers you – you might want to get changed in private, you might not like the sports kit or you might be petrified of swimming – then speak up and tell the PE teacher. They'll do what they can to help you with the problem. And if you're just nervous about stepping out of your comfort zone in a sport – for example, in your football lesson – then take the leap, kick the ball and see what happens. You never know, there might be a Messi in there somewhere!

✖ 5) It isn't the end of the world ...

I know it might feel like a huge problem that you just

CAN'T GET IT

in whatever subject is a struggle, but once you accept that perfection is impossible, then the weight can lift off your shoulders and you can start to feel a *little* bit more positive. Whether we graft through all the work in the world to improve how we do in a subject or not, the reality is that everyone is still going to have things they're better at, and things they like more.

Just because you aren't great at that one subject, the following things will still happen:

- **You'll still breathe oxygen**
- **The sun will still rise every morning and set every night**
- **People you care about will still care about you**

It's fine. Do your best – nobody will ask anything more.

⭐ 6) If there's nothing else ... be resilient

We've talked about this before, and it's one of the most important things you can do. If everything above fails, if you don't fall in love with a subject and you're dreading it every day, if you can't wait to leave because of that one classroom, there comes a time when all we have to do is get through it. Everyone has things they don't want to do and school's the same. But we can start to move our mindset from **'OH NO, I HATE THIS!'** to 'right, I don't like it, but I *can* and *will* get through it'. Give yourself something to look forward to every single day, either in or out of school, and those grey clouds following you around during the day won't appear quite as grey when you've got a cinema trip or football practice to look forward to.

'SUCCESS ISN'T ALWAYS ABOUT GREATNESS. IT'S ABOUT CONSISTENCY. CONSISTENT HARD WORK LEADS TO SUCCESS. GREATNESS WILL COME.'

Dwayne 'The Rock' Johnson – *American-Canadian actor, producer and former professional wrestler*

BUT IT WASN'T MY FAULT

Usually, the word 'behaviour' is used to talk about when people are being 'naughty', using swear words, stopping other people from learning in a classroom or generally doing stuff that they shouldn't be. But the actual definition of 'behaviour' in a dictionary is different. It's more like 'the way in which a person or animal acts',[1] and it doesn't *once* mention anyone throwing a chair, telling a teacher to 'go away',[2] fighting, bullying or generally not doing what they *should* do.

So, if behaviour is the way that people act, then we have a choice. We can either act daft or we can act sensibly and positively. What the heck does that mean, though?! It basically comes down to something that's really simple and a bit boring: following the rules.

Almost every secondary school will have a really clear set of expectations that apply to every single classroom, drama studio, workshop, sports hall, laboratory, corridor and office. You will know what they are, so that won't be a problem (they will probably be on the walls, in your homework diary or planner and in the mouths of teachers *all the time*), and that

[1] No, I'm not calling YOU an animal!
[2] NOT a good idea AT ALL!

really helps. If things are clear for you, then whether you like them or not, you know what you need to do!

Most school rules and expectations will be about your manners and your effort, too. They might all have different names, but they *really* want the same things: for you to turn up on time, put 100 per cent effort in and be kind towards everyone you meet. Doing that means you'll do well. Some schools even have reward days, stamps and postcards. They might even send letters to your parents and make phone calls home to tell them how great you are. Some will even give you free rides on the backs of unicorns surfing rainbows to take you home on a Friday afternoon.[3]

If you *don't* meet those expectations, however, that's when schools might need to use some different strategies to help you think about how your behaviour might be affecting you and other people. Nobody starts their first day *wanting* to get into trouble, of that I'm sure. Every human being – child, adult and *even* teacher – *wants* to do the right thing and be praised for it. However, the world doesn't work like a perfectly functioning cuckoo clock, where the chirping little bird pops out with a celebration chocolate every time you go to a lesson on time, work hard, get all your work done and make lots of progress. There are different types of praise and punishments/consequences or whatever else you might call it, so get ready for a bit more proper science. You ready?

[3] Unfortunately not true, which is a huge shame.

POSITIVE REINFORCEMENT

Some teachers will celebrate literally everything you do: stepping into a classroom, getting your pen out, answering a question, walking in a straight line, breathing[4] throughout the lesson. They'll *positively reinforce* the good stuff you do. You might get praised, get a high five, have a chocolate thrown to you, a postcard home – all that sort of thing. It can feel lovely, and it can motivate you to want more of that praise. It works straight away because your brain connects something you do to a reward: 'Oh, I got a lovely comment last time I answered a question well, so I'll answer another one!'

The reward is what you're actually trying to get.

If you don't do something well, you just don't get the reward. If you want to know more, have a read up about 'Pavlov's Dog' (which sounds like a Sherlock Holmes case, but is actually about rewards and reinforcing good stuff that people do).

---

[4] Definitely do this. Every lesson.

NEGATIVE REINFORCEMENT

I'm sure you can guess that this isn't quite the same as positive reinforcement, but it is similar. It's the *other* version of positive reinforcement. When you do something *wrong*, you get a negative comment or a word in your ear saying, 'Don't do that again.' However, it isn't just shouting and bawling and making you cry; negative reinforcement works so that when you *don't* do that thing wrong, the negative comment goes away. So say you're at home, and you haven't tidied the kitchen after you've made a sandwich. Your dad complains at you and it's **SOANNOYINGDADI'LLDOITJUST LETMEENJOYTHEBEAUTYOFTHISFINEJAMSANDWICHI'VE CREATEDSOLOVINGLY**. You can't enjoy the sandwich because he keeps going on about it. The next day, you come home, you make the sandwich, you clean up as you go. Your dad comes home, and **YOU CAN ENJOY THE SANDWICH!** You changed your behaviour to take away the negative comment.

Schools have punishments; we can't ignore that. Detentions, isolations, exclusions: they happen. And though they can feel really unfair, they're there so that when things do go wrong, you know that the choice you made wasn't the right one and we can stop it happening again in the future. They're the negative reinforcement side of things. Just so you're clear, these methods are what some schools use:

⋆ 1) Detention

You're told to stay at school for a time (usually up to an hour), because of something you've done (or not done – it might be not doing homework, for example). Your parents will be told, and it won't be all that enjoyable. It's frustrating, but you can get through it, right the wrong and learn from the experience. You don't *really* want to spend your valuable free time in school if you don't have to.

⋆ 2) Isolation

Have you ever heard about solitary confinement in prison? Where a particularly naughty prisoner is locked in a cell on their own for hours, a day – or even longer? Well, this is the secondary school equivalent.[5] Isolation is usually a room in a school where children will spend a day when something really quite bad has happened. You'll work on your own, away from others, and be expected to work in silence, usually. It's not a good thing, and you'll have plenty of time to think about what didn't go quite right on this occasion ...

⋆ 3) Exclusion

Has your favourite football player ever missed games because they've been suspended for doing something rash, stupid or just plain unpleasant? Exclusions work in a similar way, and

[5] To be clear, I am not equating going to school with going to prison, okay?!

way, and they happen for *very serious* things. If you're excluded, it will mean that you'll be at home for a length of time and you can't be in school. These are really, really serious, and often mean things have gone badly wrong.

If you feel that you're struggling with what's expected of you, or with any part of how you're supposed to act, use the people around you. Teachers are there to help, and even if you've had a few detentions and been in some trouble, then

it's not too late: you haven't 'spoiled it'.

It might be that you think there's something going on that's making you do certain things, and you need to be open and honest about it. Your teachers may recognise signs of special needs that you might have, and if that is the case then your school will support you to make sure it doesn't stop you from making the progress you are capable of.[6] Bouncing back from the bad stuff is what resilience is all about; there is a path back and you *can* still be a real success.

I mentioned being popular a while ago, and that pressure to be as popular as you can be, from the people around you, can lead to making bad choices, both in and out of school. In that moment, only one person can make the call and it's what every part of your life up to now has led to: is it the *right* thing to do? What's right to you depends on what your life has taught you. The law, the things and people who are precious to you and how they'll feel if you make that choice right there and then, what you've seen before and the impact these things have on people; they are all things that only you will know right there, in that moment. But think, really simply:

is it the right choice to make?

[6] Sometimes these things can take a while, so the sooner you tell someone, or someone picks it up, the better. If you're thinking this is the case, say something.

Things like smoking, illegal drugs and alcohol are just not allowed. No one in the history of Instagram has looked good with a cigarette dangling out of their mouth while declaring they're living their best life, and besides, they're illegal – drugs *for ever*, and smoking and alcohol certainly while you're at school. You might experience some peer pressure (when mates and those around you try to tempt you to do things) to try these things during secondary school, but doing things that can and will harm your (still developing) body and mind, and cause you massive problems, just isn't worth it. You're worth more than that. Have pride in yourself, make strong decisions that are right for right now *and* for your future, and walk away ... whoever is offering them to you. If you feel you're at risk of any of these things, or if you're worried about messages you're hearing about them, *please*

SPEAK UP.

It could be the best thing you ever do for yourself.

So, behaviour's a choice whether you're at secondary school, college, university or working. It's about decisions you can make, and while there are a million and one things that can affect your choices every single moment of every single day, life in secondary school is a lot easier and far more fun and enjoyable for those who *do* follow the guidelines of what's expected of them. If your choices aren't the right ones, it will frustrate you – even if it's not straight away, it will eventually. School rules are designed to let teachers teach and children learn, and everyone has a *massive* part to play in it. The benefits of getting your head down and working hard are huge, and you'll make a lot of people very proud of you by doing so. It comes down to those simple things again: work hard, be kind to everyone around you and rewards will come your way. Your dad might even make you a jam sandwich.[7] Just tell him to clean up while he's doing it.

[7] A massively underrated sandwich, honestly. Try one. You'll thank me.

THE WONDERFUL WORLD OF EXAMS

12

There probably aren't many people who saw the title of this chapter and straight away thought, *OH, YES, I JUST LOVE EXAMS!* They can be tense and pressurised, and the main reason for that is because every exam leads to an exam *result*. Of course, when they go well you'll feel like celebrating like you've just won the World Cup – jumping up and punching the air dramatically 17 times, before doing an emotional interview for a national news broadcaster to tell them how happy you are, how much you'd like to thank your family and your friends, and then swapping shirts with someone who didn't do quite so well and patting them on the head as they look quite sad about the whole thing.[1]

More and more and more, exams are built up to be *so* important. Most years, the news will report how much 'easier' they are these days than in previous years,[2] and you might have offers from colleges, sixth forms or apprenticeships for which need you to get, for example, a grade 5 in English and maths. This mix-up of pressure from everywhere can really

[1] I think this is mainly what happens in a sporting World Cup. Wouldn't really recommend it for when your first-year geography exam goes well. Save it for the end-of-school results day!

[2] From a teacher's point of view, they are definitely NOT!

mean that, even in your early years of secondary school, these exams (which might be called tests, assessments or something else) might feel really quite scary.

Not that you should be scared, of course! These are not things to be terrified of,

 they're a chance to show what you know

and, especially at the start of secondary school, they're really far, far, far, far, **FAR** more important to help show what you don't quite know just yet – so that your teachers can help you 'get it' and then show that you *do* know it next time. Maths is a good example – and my thing that I just could *not* get was long division. It was like some sort of ancient language that I just couldn't get my head around, and I felt like every time the teacher told me how to do it, some kind of witchcraft or Harry Potter-style magic was being used to bamboozle my brain. I'd think, *Yep, I get that bit. Yep, that makes complete sense. Yep, I understand that. Yep, I ... oh, crikey, what on earth just happened?!*

I just could not get my tiny little mind to understand it – I couldn't 'unlock' that bit of maths.[3] Shakespeare? Fine. Plant cells? Fine. Densely populated, less economically developed countries capital cities' birth rate? Not a problem. But long division just did not click.

Different people have different bits of school, the curriculum and lessons that they will just *get* and those that just seem like a 'nah, mate, that's not for me ...' moment. When you leave school, you'll probably find it's the same. Being an adult has good bits and bad bits,[4] and those bits in between that are sometimes good and sometimes bad. Testing and exams happen all the time, even in your job when you're older – sometimes a formal 'sit down and pass this exam', and sometimes more of a 'right, this thing I'm dealing with really is a test'. What adults need to show through those times are determination and the spirit to do the best job they possibly can – and that's why it's brilliant to learn how to gear yourself up for an exam when you're younger.

When I talk to students who don't deal all that well with exams, they're mainly scared about the word rather than the thing. If a teacher mentions a test, they freeze; if the 'end of year exam' is talked about, they panic. It's because of what they *think* it's going to be, rather than what it ends up being.

[3] It seemed to be like the big boss at the end of a level on a PlayStation game who kept destroying me so I couldn't get to the next level. Thank goodness for calculators! AND YES, THEY WERE INVENTED WHEN I WAS YOUNG, THANK YOU VERY MUCH, YOU CHEEKY SO AND SO, AND NO, THEY WEREN'T POWERED BY STEAM IN THOSE DAYS!

[4] Buying petrol and paying for it. There is nothing fun about that. Especially when it's raining and you're standing there with a hose attached to your car filling it up with liquid (apparently) and then paying LOADS OF MONEY for it. Hopefully you will end up driving an electric car and we can forget the whole petrol thing altogether!

People seem to think that all exams are to catch you out – but they're not!

The questions will be things that have been covered in your lessons. Maybe not just yesterday's lesson, and you might have to stretch your brain to pull it out from the very back shelf of your knowledge (like that jar of 'something' that everyone's grandma has in their kitchen cupboard that's coated in dust and has been there for years), but it will be from what you've been taught. The questions might need you to think a little bit differently to how you would if you were learning it in a normal lesson, but you know this stuff! I always say two things to people going into exams (and if the answer to both is 'yes', then they usually feel better).

Mr Burton's questions that will make you feel a little, tiny, microscopic bit better:

1) Do you want to do well?
2) Have you worked hard to prepare?

Often, those people who were terrified going into the exam come out high-fiving down the corridors or doing a sliding knee celebration across the dining hall because they have worked hard and they know –

they have that *FEELING*

– that all that hard work in lessons and at home has paid off. Turning a page over to reveal page after page of questions that you know how to do is a great feeling. It makes you feel much more confident for the next exam, and the next one, and you can build strong, confident foundations for the future.

In any exam, you might not be the one deciding what questions to answer, but you are *definitely* the one who decides how well you do.

'Exam' is just a word

– like how some people don't really like the words 'fire', 'homework' and 'rain' because of what they make you think of. Actually, fire keeps us warm when we're out camping and it's **FREEZING**; I'm sure you can remember at least one piece of homework that you *really* enjoyed doing; and rain can be so beautiful and magical in the middle of summer when it's been **BOILING** for **WEEKS**, and you can dance around on the decking at the back of the house pretending you're in a music video on YouTube. The point is that we attach certain preconceptions[5] to exams that aren't really true – if you approach them in the right way, with the right attitude, then you will be absolutely fine.

[5] An idea we get in our heads just because it's what we've been *told* to think or because of what we've experienced in the past.

'FEAR IS JUST AN EMOTION. YOU CAN'T LET YOUR EMOTIONS RULE YOUR LIFE ... YOU JUST HAVE TO DO WHAT YOU WOULD DO IF YOU WEREN'T AFRAID AND THEN GO FROM THERE.'

Venus Williams - *American tennis player*

MR BURTON'S KEY EXAM TIPS

⭐ 1) Don't stress too much

Remember that this is not the end of the world. Things can go wrong; they can (if they need to) be redone.

⭐ 2) Breathe deeply

In. Out. In. Out. In. Out.

⭐ 3) Go for a run, a swim or a walk

Exercise and fresh air are good for stress – and you're not going to be the best version of you and do a cracking job in an exam if you can't relax.

✦ 4) Plan

Plan for how many exams you have by making a really clear wall chart telling you what you're going to revise and when (including listing the actual bits of subjects you're going to revise).

✦ 5) Calm

Make sure you have a quiet, calm place to revise, away from mess and clutter. Turn the telly off, put your phone away and remove any other distractions so you can't be procrastinating.[6]

✦ 6) Plan in your breaks

Exam time is about working hard, yes, but it's also about pacing yourself! Would a marathon

---

[6] Finding anything other than your actual work to do, just to avoid doing your work. For example, plaiting the dog's hair, learning how to Irish dance from a YouTube video or making an industrial-sized batch of chocolate brownies.

runner do 43 miles the night before a run? No, not at all. They'd rest up, have a sensible meal and think through the main bits they need to remember for the following day. If they didn't spend time doing that, they wouldn't even have a chance of finishing, let alone doing a good job. Exams are the same – pace yourself, think about what you want success to look like and then do everything you can to make that happen. But don't hurt yourself to get there; returning to what I said at the top, show what you know, but just as important is what you don't know *just* yet.

✬ 7) Use the right resources

Your teachers will give you some, but also use other bits and pieces that you find online (but check with your teachers how good they are first).

✬ 8) Revise together

Revise with a friend to make it seem a little bit easier. Test each other and help to make

the knowledge sink in by talking it through,
writing it down and striving hard to remember
it with someone else who's in the same boat,
understands what's needed and needs to
work on similar things!

THE BIG MOVE

13

It's not just exams that can be stressful; other things in your life can mean that you go through changes that you can't control. One might be moving from one school to another. There can be a thousand different reasons why you might need to move to a different secondary school even though you've already started at one. You might move house, your family situation might change, you might just not get on very well where you started and fancied a change. Whatever the reason, this is the bit for you!

How do you feel about the move?

You might be excited about a fresh start or you could feel like the world is ending and you're absolutely distraught that your mum or dad chose to take that job 300 miles away from all your mates. Either way: you *can* and *will* still be a brilliant success. The first, and most important, thing for you is to try your best to be as positive about the move as you possibly can – whether it's the first, second, third or fourth time you've changed schools.

I mentioned before that every teacher in every single town in every country, on every planet,[1] wants to help you. Schools don't set up to stop children making successes of themselves; they are places where young people are encouraged to be brilliant and faaabulous. So moving from Glasgow to Sydney to New York to Cardiff might feel tough (and it would be, especially if you're walking), but your school will help you settle in and build yourself back up again. You might be feeling a lot of anger about it – 'Why do I have to move again?', 'Why can't I be *normal*?'[2], 'Will I *ever* get to make any friends?' – but talk to people and find your 'go-to' guys/gals again.

I still love it when students come and share any woes they have with me, and there are plenty of reasons for it: firstly, I can try to help, and often can (and even if I can't, I'll know a person who can); and secondly, I like it when people come to chat because I know from personal experience that sharing a problem really does help. Everyone needs their 'go-to' person to have a whinge or a moan or a little bit of a cry[3] with, so don't

[1] Apart from Jupiter. The teachers there are 'orrible. Don't let your dad take a job there. Even if the money's good, the journey there would kill you, it's made of gas so you couldn't actually stand up and, most disturbingly, it doesn't have any Internet access or phone signal.
[2] We've talked about that – remember, nobody's 'normal'!
[3] Oh, and by 'cry' I mean a PROPERLY UGLY CRY, as if you've been chopping onions and watching a romantic comedy at the same time and dropped a tin of tomatoes on your foot. (Just to be safe, if you're chopping onions: MAKE SURE YOU'RE SAFE WITH THE KNIFE AND CERTAINLY DON'T WATCH A FILM AT THE SAME TIME! Are you *crackers*?!)

feel you're the only one in a school who's not feeling 100 per cent.

There might be another reason why you're moving, such as a permanent exclusion (where your behaviour at your previous school has meant that you've been told you have to leave) or a managed transfer or move (where you try another school out for a period of time to see if you get along better there). Whatever the reason is, follow these steps for moving school and you'll be fine. It's a lot like diving into a swimming pool from a massive ten-metre diving board ...

✦ 1) Get your swimming kit on!

You can't go swimming without your trunks on,[4] can you? Get your stuff ready for your new school and turn up looking

ready
for ACTION.

---

[4] And please don't try to. Bad idea.

✦ 2) Just *know* that you're going to land just fine

Try to be positive and open-minded. You might not want to be there, but you are. You're ten metres up, there's a big queue behind you and the only way down is to jump. If you've already decided you're going to land on the side of the pool rather than *in* the pool and make a big mess, then you're more likely to. But

YOU WON'T!

Give your school a chance, and more often than not, you'll find good stuff about it really quickly. If you've already decided you hate it and it's awful before you've even worked out a single equation in maths, what chance are you giving it?!

✦ 3) Ask people how deep it is

Talk to people. Get the low-down and *ze information*; get to grips with where to be and when. Try to build those foundations of relationships with the new people, and make sure that you're telling your folks what's good and what's not so good when you get home.

✦ 4) Dive into it

Then just jump. You'll find that the first tiny little nanosecond is terrifying, but from then on, you'll take to it like a duck to water.

SPLASH!

Leap into the Fu

ing
ture

BUTCHER, BAKER OR CANDLESTICK MAKER:

WHAT SHOULD I DO WHEN I GROW UP?

14

The future can seem a fairly terrifying thing when you think about it for too long. If you search for 'the future' online, it'll conjure up all sorts of things to do with flying cars, robots serving you breakfast and living on other planets. But that's not the future we're thinking about in this bit. We're talking about *your* future. What impact are you going to have on the world around you, and how are you going to influence things?

You might think, *Steady on, I'm only a child*! And you would be right to! You've still got most of your life ahead of you and don't have to sign up for a mortgage or decide what your plans for your retirement are just yet. School will help you *start* to think about things that gently swerve you into a certain direction, where you *could* do that job in the future if you *wanted*, but should help you keep your options wide enough so that you don't *have* to be a professional extreme-cake decorator or a travelling tightrope walker even if you want to be that *right* now. You need to arrive (and leave) knowing that you have a few different directions you could go in.

Remember, even today was the future yesterday, so think about how you can have an impact on the short-term as well as deciding how you want to change the world when you're a little older.

LITTLE STEPS

Nobody in school is going to say,

'YOU MUST BE A DOCTOR!'

purely because you did well on a test in biology in your first week back after the summer holidays. Teachers will see if you're particularly talented in an area – they might even have a word with you about it or give you things to do to help develop your interest in that subject – but they won't force you. Who does that help? It'll switch you off like a smashed light bulb – your interest will reduce to almost zero overnight and they'll have made you not like their subject. And remember, teachers want you to enjoy their subject; they love that thing – whether it's English, maths, science, PE, history or whatever – and they want you to as well!

If you like a subject and think it *might possibly potentially could be maaaybe* for you, then be open and ask the questions you need answering ... but don't worry about it if you're good at something that you don't really like – that might come in time!

CAREER GOALS

A goal is a fairly big thing. Imagine you're about to take a penalty in the World Cup Final, and a goal is staring at you. It's *massive* – and really wide. At this point, your goals probably are, too. Maybe from the age of five (like me), you have been absolutely sure that you wanted to be a train driver (mainly thanks to *Thomas the Tank Engine* in my case). That was a goal without any real understanding of why and how. I certainly didn't understand that trains don't actually have friendly little faces and talk to you. If your goals right now are stuck in the past (like mine were), it might be time to start thinking a little bit more about what you enjoy. Research, read and look into the type of things you like and develop your thoughts around starting to pave the road to your future.

Don't think that I'm saying career goals are a bad idea, even early on. Definitely not! If you're proud as punch about what you want to do and wear your bright yellow **'FUTURE MIDWIFE'** T-shirt on a Saturday afternoon, that's brilliant. It may very well happen, and I really hope it does. It's just important to remember these top tips when you're setting those goals, so that you really enjoy being at school and don't just see it as a stepping stone to doing a job ...

⭐ 1) Try not to pin it down to one job

It's hard sometimes, because (like I just said) some people will want to be a particular thing. Whether that's a butcher, baker or indeed a candlestick maker, ask yourself: why do I want to do that? Try to pin it down to what you enjoy doing and the things you enjoy learning about, the things you're good at and what people see in you. Focus on those things because you enjoy excelling in them, not because you're keen as a cucumber to do it so you can pay your bills in a few years' time! It might end up being a hobby and you might end up with a career that doesn't even exist yet. Who knows?!

⭐ 2) Research and dream big!

If you're a fan of a subject, don't just settle on liking it. That's not enough. Be thirsty. Be ambitious. Go and look into what amazing jobs you *could* do (remember, you don't have to when it comes to it) with that subject that you like and/or that you're good at. Being good at science doesn't just mean you could be a scientist. You could be ...

**a nuclear biologist
a doctor
a meteorologist
an astronaut
an oceanographer
a penguinologist**

a toxicologist,
a space lawyer
a teacher
or you could be a professional ice dancer.

There's nothing wrong with dreaming, and research is a good thing. Be well-informed and do your reading. When you meet the careers guidance person at school, they'll help you to craft your dreams and find a pathway to what you're going to be. It can't always be that everyone who loves science becomes an astronaut, but what is the world without goals and dreams?!

✮ 3) Don't stop learning

Every single day you spend in secondary school will help you when you finally arrive at your career. Every time you meet someone new, every time you hold a door for someone, every time you're let down by a friend or something goes wrong. They're valuable lessons, and they'll help you become the person you ultimately will be. It's vital that you put the hard work in and take every chance to make sure you're the best version of yourself every single day, so that when you eventually *do* need to take the plunge and decide which career is for you, you've made sure that every available door is open.

FOLLOWING YOUR PASSIONS

My goodness me, this is so important.

Do what you ENJOY doing.

Please. Don't give yourself a really miserable time at school by telling yourself that you need to focus more in one subject just because that's definitely the job you're going to do. That's not fair on you and it's going to make you really sad in the long-term. If you enjoy performing, then get involved in performances; if you're sporty, play sport; if you're passionate about fighting for the environment, then join the school's campaign group on climate change. Do what you enjoy and find new things at secondary school that you didn't even know existed, let alone enjoyed, because the world is wide and wonderful and there will be lots that you can do, love doing and are fantastic at. If you're glued to your phone[1] and love taking pictures and videos, then you might be the world's next massive film producer or world-famous photographer. Who knows unless you give it a go and share your work with others?[2] Someone might see your work, think you're brilliant, and you could look back and think of that picture you took of a sunset on your way to your first day at school being one of the most important moments of your life. Thinking of the future involves trying things out – if you don't know what it's like, then how will you ever know if it's for you?!

OPTIONS/PARENTAL PRESSURE

At some point in secondary school – though not during the first year, so don't worry – you'll make some decisions about subjects you want to study in the next stage of your life.

---

[1] Don't do that. Not metaphorically, but *definitely* not literally. It'll break your phone and leave you with an ear covered in glue.
[2] Safely, and in the right places, with the right people.

This is when you'll probably talk to a careers advisor, maybe have an interview with some other teachers, and think about what you're going to do in the next bit. They're usually called 'options', and are important in carrying on paving that road to the future for you. It's a big moment, but remember: this isn't the final choice you'll ever make, and you are not choosing your career at this point.

Certain jobs will benefit from you having certain qualifications – and it is definitely worth doing your research to see what you'd need if you do actually fancy being a doctor, an architect, a classical musician or a marine biologist – but don't make choices that stop you being a widely qualified human being in a couple of years' time.

Your options are, remember, your options. Your parents might really, really want you to be a business owner, a skydiving instructor, a member of the military, a teacher, a boxer or a travelling salesman of woodwind instruments, but remember:

THESE ARE YOUR OPTIONS!

It's about listening to all the people who care about you and want the best for you, talking it through, asking the questions you need to ask, and making the choices that are right for *you*. They want the best for you, but more than that, they want you to be happy and achieving.

KEEP YOUR OPTIONS OPEN FOR AS LONG AS POSSIBLE

Nobody's asking you to write your future career on a piece of paper, lock it in a treasure chest and then reopen it in a decade to check whether you actually did what you said you wanted to. The truth is, people change their minds – more than you'd ever think, to be honest – so it's really important that while you think of the future as being something that is yours to go out and do a fantastic job at acing, on your way there you enjoy yourself, learn lots of interesting things from interesting subjects and then make a decision at the right time, when you've got all the information available to you. You may fancy university now, but that might change, and vice versa. You could develop a passion for breeding guinea pigs in your final year of school after finding an abandoned family of them at a bus stop. Who knows what life's going to throw at us? Use secondary school as the chance to get ready and prepared for a brilliant and bright career in something you adore doing.

And also, if you think that because something isn't great right now your future is ruined, remember that it's never too late to put the work in and change the direction you're going in.

Never.
Ever.
Ever.

Of course, it's better if everything runs smoothly, but there are a million different reasons why things might not have gone well for a day, a week, a month or even years, but there's always a way back. There is always a moment when your brain decides things have to change, and you come back fighting to claim your future. It may not be today, it may not be tomorrow, but if things aren't great right now, there's a path back ... and you *can* do it. Even Albert Einstein's[3] teachers thought he was a bad student at school. He ended up being thought of as one of the finest brains ever to walk the face of the planet, despite his teachers never, ever thinking that would happen.

[3] The pretty clever scientist gentleman with big hair!

'YOU'VE GOTTEN THIS FAR, YOU GOT THIS!'

Stormzy – *British rapper and singer*

OFF

YOU

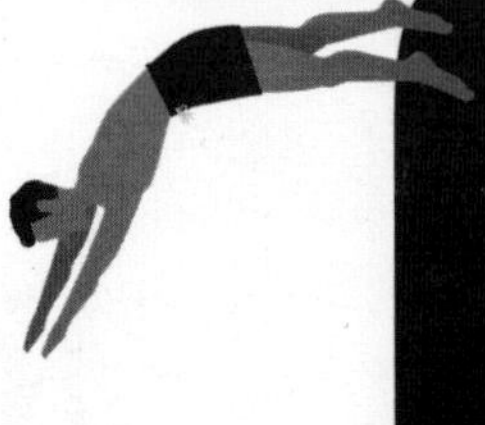

GO

I'm writing this the day after our students from last year have picked up their GCSE results after fiiive lonnng yeeears of being a huge part of the school. This is a day that feels a little bit strange for all sorts of people. For everyone who's involved in the final school exams – teachers, you, your parents, your grandma who's promised you a fiver for every top grade you get – it will seem like a thousand years from the minute you left school after your last exam (shirt covered in pen from your friends' messages of 'kindness', tears streaming down your face even though you've tried so hard not to cry and put your throat muscles through a huge workout for the whole final assembly saying goodbye) to the moment you're handed a brown envelope.

Your teacher will smile and say 'Good luck' but you won't hear a thing. You'll try to smile but your tummy will be jumping around like a jelly on a trampoline being dragged down a bumpy road, and then it's *the moment*. You've thought about it a million billion times, and here it is. These are the ones you've been waiting for. At this stage, what will go through your head (and what will already have gone through your head a load of times throughout that summer) are these things:

- If I *haven't* done well, then that's just awful

- If I *haven't* done well, then I have absolutely no future in the way that I thought I would

- If I *have* done well, then have I made the right choice for what's next?

- What will people *think*, however I have done?

- Should I open them *now* or wait?

Once you've got them, opened them and had a quick look – in between breathless, blinkless moments of panic, when your eyes are watering a little bit and you feel like every single eye in the room is on you[1] – then you can start to plan your path into the next bit of your life. Before you do that (or even think about that), though, you need to take some time for you. The approach to this day will feel like it lasted for ever:[2] the hard work you've done getting ready for them, thinking about them and chatting about the papers and grade boundaries with your friends, and then newspapers and websites, radio and TV stations blaring out about them for the last week,

[1] They're not, by the way; they're much too worried about how they've done themselves!

[2] At that stage, it will feel like you first heard the word 'exam results day' the moment you were born and have never not been thinking about it.

giving hourly countdowns. It will feel like a really heavy iron suit of armour from the olden days that knights used to fight in, which you can only strip off once your own battle is won.[3]

Afterwards, there are some other things to make sure you do (and don't do):

✦ 1) Don't compare yourself to others

You've done your best. That's all you can do. Thinking, *Well, if I'd got this extra mark here then I could do that college course with Cassie and she didn't even revise and I know she's got a tutor so it isn't even fair* ... does you no good at all.

✦ 2) Be angry ... then be proactive

It's fine to be disappointed. If you haven't got what you wanted, or what the college or apprenticeship you were looking forward to wanted you to have, then it's normal to feel like you've taken a punch to the stomach. You've got two choices then: accept it or fight back. Plan the next few months and chalk off accomplishments day by day, week by week, month by month. What's your goal, and how are you going to make it happen? Just because it didn't go right *this*

---

[3] This is a metaphor. Do not wear chain mail, iron-plated suits or anything else medieval to pick up your exam results. It is not necessary. It is also probably not a good idea to take a horse with you to collect them, given the 'mess' they could make of the school's reception area with the lovely carpet. You know what I mean ... ahem. Eugh.

time does not define the rest of your life. Get out there and put it right.

⭐ 3) Enjoy it – and be proud

If things have gone well, then don't feel you have to keep it really quiet because some others are a bit fed up with what's happened. You have **GRAFTED** and **WORKED** and (probably) **CRIED** for this single piece of paper folded lovingly into a brown envelope by your teacher, and now you deserve your chance to be proud of yourself. There will have been times in your life when you felt as if you didn't fit in, when your best wasn't ever going to be good enough, when you couldn't even imagine that results as good as these would be **YOURS**, but take a second to take this bit in: they are yours. Nobody can take them away and they are worth celebrating, so get your swimming stuff on and jump into the paddling pool in the back garden!

⭐ 4) Ask yourself: where do these fit in?

Now you've got them, how do they work for you? If you wanted to do an apprenticeship, do they get you where you want to be? If you're looking at going to college or sixth form for more 'classroom' studying, do they do the business to get you there? Have that chat with yourself nice and early, and if you need to look at resitting any, then make it really clear to your next place that you're happy to do that. And those future plans that you have – where do they fit in there? If that envelope (and what's inside it) ticks the boxes you've been asked to tick to move into the next bit of your education, then great. If it doesn't, then what needs to happen *right now* so that you can do it as soon as possible?

⭑ 5) Talk. To. People.

I can't shout this loudly enough. Imagine I'm **SHOUTING THIS REALLY LOUDLY, OKAY?**

Talk.
To.
People.
At.
School!

It's quite likely that this will be one of the last times you'll
be able to use everyone at school. It's very likely that, in the
busy, buzzing chaos of results day, most people you need will
be there in one place. From your head teacher to your head
of year, and from your English teacher to your careers advisor
who told you a couple of years ago that your goal of being an
astronaut by the time you're 17 wasn't going to happen:

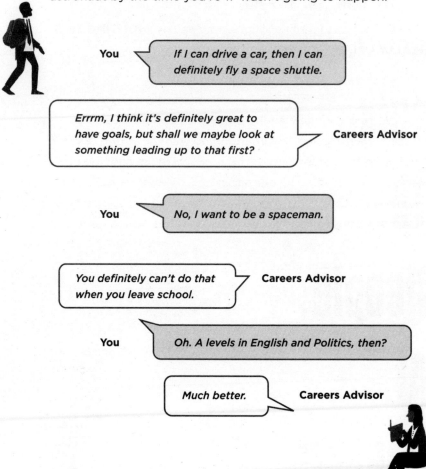

You — *If I can drive a car, then I can definitely fly a space shuttle.*

Errrm, I think it's definitely great to have goals, but shall we maybe look at something leading up to that first? — Careers Advisor

You — *No, I want to be a spaceman.*

You definitely can't do that when you leave school. — Careers Advisor

You — *Oh. A levels in English and Politics, then?*

Much better. — Careers Advisor

The fact that they're all together is great for a few reasons. Firstly, if it's gone well, get someone to slow-motion film you running down a line of them high-fiving dramatically, and then set it to dramatic music later before sharing it with your friends with an inspirational quote about hard work.[4]

Faaar more important though, is that you've got a lot of very brilliant brains in one room that have all got one interest at the centre of them: you. Whatever your question is, go and see the person who can help. Want to know the grade boundaries in maths? You know where to go! Think you've made the wrong choice about which college to go to and are worried your decision to study a three-year course on basket weaving and flower arranging was the wrong option? Speak to the careers advisor! Is it all too much and you don't understand what's on your paper and what all the different numbers mean? Grab your brilliant teaching assistant who's been supporting you for five years! Want to have a good old cry, as you just feel rubbish and don't know why? Go to that person who's been there for you and have that good old cry!

[4] Something like: 'What comes easy won't last. What lasts won't come easy.'

⭐ 6) Own it

You have no choice about this one, but it's a state-of-mind thing. Your envelope is your envelope, and whatever is in there is in there. Good, bad, ugly or beautiful, it's yours. However you feel about it, be open, honest and realistic about it and get out there, use it as a starting point and don't be afraid to be proud of what you did. Exam results can be a day in someone's life when growing up becomes a reality for the first time, and if you've not been working hard enough for a few years and knew it really, then use today as a springboard. You might feel elated and want more of these days – in that case, go and get more – but you might feel heartbroken and miserable and don't *ever* want to feel that way again – in that case, remember that feeling and plan how you're going to do things differently so that it never happens again.

⭐ 7) And PLEASE LET PEOPLE KNOW!

Your team – whoever's in it – have been waiting for this day for the same amount of time as you have. Your mum, dad, brother, sister, auntie, uncle, cousin, grandma, grandad, nanna, your mum's auntie's cousin, the lady in the shop you go to on your way to school, your boss at your Saturday job: they're all living this day too! They've woken up this morning and probably haven't slept well. They're staring at their phone, wondering if it's broken. They're texting people 'just to check messages are getting through' and **THEY WANT TO KNOW HOW IT WENT!** Make sure you don't forget your squad. Text them, call them, send a telegram,[5] hire an aeroplane and fly a banner across the sky, pay for a whole-page advert in the local newspaper or even (which, to be honest, seems much easier) just go and see them. They're proud of you, they care about you (and your future), and they're there to celebrate the good with you (and cushion you if it's less good).

Overall, the beautiful, confusing, topsy-turvy chaos of results day is one that you can plan in loads of detail for, but all of your planning can quickly unravel the moment something happens that you didn't expect (good or bad ... or even just weird – if Starbucks is closed on your way into school, for example).[6] It's a day you're likely to remember for ever – one of happiness, pride, tears, sadness, goodbyes, and it's the day when you become clear about the next step. After today you probably won't see some of the people you've spent years and years with (ever since nursery, when that boy nipped you and you still haven't forgiven him), and – added to the **ENVELOPE OF MYSTERY** – that's a lot to take in.

By this time, there's little point in saying it, as the ink on the paper already in the envelope is already printed ... but good luck, fingers crossed and go out and own the day and your results, and in a few short hours, the future will be here!

[5] Ask your grandparents. Like emails but before emails existed. And the Queen still sends British people one on their hundredth birthday. Fact.
[6] In that case the world has definitely ended. It *never* closes.

CONCL

USION

So that's that. Is that *everything* you'll ever need to navigate your way through secondary school? I doubt it. I think this book would need to be 856,439,564,389 pages long (and weigh the same as a killer whale just after it's been for a rather large lunch) if it was going to cover every single little thing that people YOUR AGE have EVER been through in their first couple of years as they move on up.

Of course, there's more to come. That's life! It's beautiful and scary and lets you down and picks you up and makes you cry (for good and bad reasons), and you're entering that bit of life when you'll feel everything just that little bit more. And does that make things easier for the big move? Naaah. What fun would *that* be if life was going to be easy?! The ups would just feel 'meh' or 'whatever', and you wouldn't feel the things you're going to feel in only a short time.

I see hundreds of people starting secondary school every year and I always make a really clear point, in that first assembly we have together, of asking them to look around. Look at the room, the other children, the teachers. Take in the smell of the place. Look at yourself. Why do I do that? Simple. Because things change so quickly. Adults will always talk about school days being 'the best days of your life', and children usually make a strange noise through their nose that sounds a bit like a mildly angered horse sneezing (try it). I hate to be *another* one of *those*, but the reason I ask people to look around is because of that. It'll fly by so quickly, and there's a really strong chance that you will miss it so, so much.

There will be laughter, love, smiles, smells, spots and horrible moments when you realise there's no lock on the toilet door. There'll be tantrums, tears, times you'll never forget and times you wish the ground could swallow your entire body up, and others you'll desperately want to forget. There'll be fun, frustration, friends, fancying people and feeling, well, just ... weird. There'll be writing, reading, talking, calculating, running, jumping, throwing, learning, practising, failing ... and succeeding.

There will, of course, be dark days. Life doesn't hand you everything you want with a smile and a polite 'There you go sir/madam ...' every time, like a waiter in a fine restaurant bringing you your favourite pizza **FOR FREE**. We have to understand, dear reader, that you will do silly things, make a load of mistakes and most certainly say things to people that will make you cringe straight after and wish you could swallow the words back down again. Just so you know: you can't. Sorry!

But let's not pretend everyone isn't experiencing the same thing. We *have* to accept that, with everything that's going on around us at the time in our lives that we start secondary school, it is **FINE** to occasionally do things wrong, and it's definitely also fine to say a few things wrong, but we should always, always, always do our best to be kind.

Maya Angelou (an AMAZING and VERY BUSY American singer, dancer, actor, writer, poet and activist campaigning for equality for black people in America) said,

'TRY TO BE A RAINBOW IN SOMEONE'S CLOUD.'

Maya Angelou – *American singer, dancer, actor, writer, poet and activist*

Let's open doors in corridors, smile and say good morning and help that new boy who's just started in your school and is looking a bit lonely at lunch. Let's spend the time at secondary school being an architect for the adult version of you. Architects don't just draw one plan; they draw a load and let you decide which one you want for your new fancy house. One might have a swimming pool and one might not; one might have an underground lair where you can pretend to be Batman and one might not (though that would be cool). The point is that you can only be you. Spend time finding your way and make the mistakes you need to (and will) make.

But above all else,

work hard
and be nice.

Simple really, isn't it?

Resources

BBC Bitesize
A free online resource to help with homework, revision and learning.
https://www.bbc.co.uk/bitesize

Bullying
Online advice on bullying and mental health.
https://www.bullying.co.uk

Childline
A counselling service for children and young people. Their website has lots of advice, articles, games and message boards on everything from mental health and money, to school and bullying.
https://www.childline.org.uk

Mind
Mind is a mental health charity. In the link below you can find information about mental health, well-being and how to find support.
https://www.mind.org.uk/information-support/for-young-people/

Sources

In order of appearance:

Yousafzai, Malala. *I Am Malala: The Story of the Girl Who Stood Up for Education and Was Shot by the Taliban* (London: Little Brown, 2013).

Guardiola, Josep. Quote reproduced in '50 Best Managers in World Football Right Now.' *Bleacher Report*, 25 September 2012 *https://bleacherreport.com/articles/1345574-50-best-world-football-managers-right-now#slide0,* accessed 15 November 2019.

Parton, Dolly. *Twitter.com.* 8 April 2015. *https://twitter.com/DollyPartonstatus/585890099583397888,* accessed 15 November 2019.

Wek, Alek. '*Alek Wek:* "You don't have to go with the crowd."' The *Guardian*, 28 March 2014 (interview) *https://www.theguardian.com/fashion/2014/mar/28/alek-wek-interview-sudanese-supermodel-dont-have-to-go-with-the-crowd,* accessed 15 November 2019.

Obama, Michelle. *People* magazine's '40th Anniversary' issue, 20 October 2014.

Hawking, Stephen. Quote reproduced in 'Stephen Hawking in His Own Words', *The New York Times*, 14 March 2018 *https://www.nytimes.com/2018/03/14/world/europe/ stephen-hawking-quotes.html*, accessed 15 November 2019.

Johnson, Dwayne. *Twitter.com.* 8 June 2012. *https://twitter.com/TheRock/status/211054285432160257*, accessed 15 November 2019.

Stormzy. *Twitter.com.* 17 May 2016. *https://twitter.com/stormzy/status/732509806838358016*, accessed 15 November 2019.

Williams, Venus. 'Venus Williams on Work-Life Balance: "There's No Such Thing as Real Balance."' *Parade,* 28 October 2019 (interview) *https://parade.com/941358/jerylbrunner/venus-williams-work-life-balance/*, accessed 15 November 2019.

Angelou, Maya. *Letter to My Daughter* (New York: Random House, 2008).